Living Off the Sea

Living Off the Sea

BONNIE O'BOYLE

A Sunrise Book · **E. P. Dutton** · **New York**

LIBRARY OF CONGRESS CATALOGING IN PUBLICATION DATA
O'Boyle, Bonnie.   Living off the sea.
   "A Sunrise book."
   Bibliography: p.   Includes index.
   1. Boat living.   I. Title.
GV777.7.035 1978   796.1'2   77-26046
ISBN: 0-87690-284-0
Published simultaneously in Canada by Clarke, Irwin &
Company Limited, Toronto and Vancouver

10 9 8 7 6 5 4 3 2 1

First Edition

*To my best friends, my parents.
And to John Jameson who listened
to the problems.*

ACKNOWLEDGMENTS

Without the cheerfulness and encouragement of Jeff Hammond and Oliver Moore of *Motor Boating & Sailing*, where some of this material first appeared, this book would have ranked somewhere between the Edsel and Alf Landon as a working proposition. Thanks, also, to the staff of *Rudder*, where it all started. Many liveaboards helped write this book, with their ideas and suggestions. I'd particularly like to thank the members of the Seven Seas Cruising Association and the Ocean Cruising Club. Esther Bradley deserves a special thank-you, as does the staff of the Calvert School. To *Arabella*, the fairest six-meter of all, I owe the idea.

CONTENTS

IS THIS THE LIFE FOR YOU?

Right now, at least 200,000 Americans live on boats. Admittedly, no one has taken a census, but that's a reasonable estimate based on the percentage of marina slips occupied by liveaboard boats, plus allowance for those who are cruising full time from place to place.

It is a staggering figure, considering that just ten years ago the liveaboard life-style was pretty uncommon, something that existed in small numbers in isolated pockets like Southern California and Florida. Now it pops up all over. For instance, I live in a suburban Philadelphia town on the upper reaches of the Delaware River in Pennsylvania, a small-boat area that's semi-industrialized. At the marina across the river in New Jersey where I kept my own sloop, I was surprised to find two liveaboard boats on the same dock. One was occupied by a three-year veteran of the liveaboard life, the other by a comparative newcomer who was starting his first summer of living on his cruiser. When I sold my old sloop last year, it was—ironically—to a liveaboard couple who had traveled from California looking for a wood boat they could afford. I would have considered *Arabella* with her eight-foot beam and long overhangs too cramped for life on board, but she was just the thing the young couple wanted and when last I heard from them in the Caribbean, she was a success in all ways. The moral is that living on boats, no longer an odd phenomenon in small numbers, can be done anywhere on almost any kind of boat.

Now 200,000 people equals the population of a small city, and these folks could fill a city not only by numbers but by occupations. They're a true cross section of America, representing almost every profession, every class, every level of education. There are lawyers, bankers, even millionaires living on boats. There are high-school dropouts, artists, college professors, mechanics, musicians, and at least one psychiatrist who has an office on his boat. And they live on every kind of floating home, from 24-foot production sloops to proud 100-foot custom yachts. There's no such thing as a "typical" liveaboard. For instance, take the following four families: They have different expectations, different backgrounds, different life-styles, but they have in common a love for the freedom, camaraderie, and adventure of boat life.

The Voyaging Life. They're a handsome couple. She's 26, deeply tanned with shoulder-length blonde hair. He's a 32-year-old Yale graduate who works as a free-lance TV producer. Ask them why they relish the liveaboard life on their converted 100-foot Baltic trader and they'll tell you that the boat is "instant waterfront property."

They bought her about three years ago for $25,000 in Denmark, then set about converting her at a cost of about $10,000, ending up with an apartment-size interior 76 feet by 21 feet. That's enough to handle all the friends they like to take along. Fortunately, they have a lot of friends because the boat takes a minimum of four people to handle her eight sails and requires a crew of eight to cross an ocean. That may be the major disadvantage, says the husband, "It's sometimes a nuisance having eight people in your home!"

So far, their home has carried them 20,000 miles, across the Atlantic, up the coast to Maine, and down through the Caribbean islands in the winter. In this case it was the wife who talked the husband into living below the waterline. She had spent a few years in the Islands ferrying cargo around in her old boat, another but smaller Baltic trader. He's happily adapted to the life, now says he regrets not doing it sooner: "I had apartments in New York for years, and I like going home to something that doesn't look like the inside of an icebox."

No Retirement Village. "As you get older, you like to pull in some of the loose strings and simplify your life," says the 70-year-old doctor, still practicing medicine in the Connecticut town that's been his home for 37 years. The only difference is that he now commutes to his office—just a block and a half away—from a 38-foot trawler instead of the big house he and his wife had been rattling around in. The decision to move was made about nine years ago, when their last child left the nest.

"Now everybody knows that it's fun to live on a boat in the summer," says the doctor, "but we decided to try it for one winter. We liked it so well, we've been aboard ever since."

Sure, there have been changes: "You're all through with big parties, which we didn't like anyway." And though the couple lost their big garden, they have a miniature replacement in the flower boxes on their dock. Other than missing a bathtub occasionally, they have no regrets. They couldn't slip the docklines with a house, they say, and take off for Florida or Canada as they do with their boat.

In an age when young people are opting for alternate lifestyles, the doctor can smile and say, "I think my two sons both envy me."

A Woman Handles It Alone. "You can't realize how beautiful nature is until you live on a boat. We never miss a sunset," the 59-year-old widow told me when I visited her 36-foot Chris-Craft in St. Petersburg, Florida. Ten years ago, the thought that she would someday live on a boat was about as remote to her as energy shortages. Back then, she lived a typical suburban life outside Philadelphia, taking care of a family and working part time for a bank.

The catalyst was her husband's heart problems, which forced him into an early retirement and discussion of a longtime dream of his—to live aboard. They decided to try it and walked out of their house with little except some clothes, a few keepsakes, and the keys to the Chris. It was a staggering change for a middle-class housewife, but in 1976, when her husband died after eight years of living aboard, his widow never considered moving back on land. She and her 14-year-old son both enjoy the boat too much.

They also enjoy fitting into their "neighborhood." The widow was den mother for a Cub Scout troop that met on the boat; she handles props for a theatrical group; she has turned a neglected 1,500-foot stretch of municipal land into a garden and has spent days cleaning ducks caught in oil spills off the Florida coast.

Simplifying her life, stripping possessions down to essentials once bothered her, but no more. "I can go to galleries and look at *things* if I want to. That way, I can appreciate them, but I don't have to find a place to put them," she says matter-of-factly.

For a few years, her eldest son was a second-generation live-aboard, on a Wheeler just a few slips from his mother's Chris. But he moved into an apartment when he married. Not Mom. If she remarries, she says firmly, there'd be no moving to a house—"Maybe to another boat!"

The Freewheeling California Life. They moved aboard the boat temporarily—to save money. That was in 1970 when Southern California was hit by a slump in the electronics industry and the husband in this couple—an engineer—was laid off for a time. But they "got hooked" on living aboard and when he went back to work, they didn't move back to land.

Instead, they started looking for a larger version of their 29-foot sailboat and settled for the bare hull of a 42-foot design.

It took them three and a half years to turn this fiber-glass overgrown bathtub into a cruising home.

During those years, the husband worked four days a week at his engineering office, the rest of the time on the boat. His wife worked full time on the hull, fiber-glassing, sanding, painting, and buying materials.

Finally, they moved aboard their larger home with relief: "It gives us the freedom we enjoy in an atmosphere we thrive on," says the wife, adding that they don't care to move back to a house or apartment—"too immobile."

They've watched friends try the same life-style, sometimes successfully and sometimes not. One family moved back on land because they missed their piano, another "because of the children." Our boatbuilding couple think the latter is the worst excuse for failure of all. Their year-old daughter was born on the boat—at a doctor's dock—and with the help of some ingenious slings and other modifications to the boat, thrives there. "She can move around the boat better than she can on land," says her mother, and they wait for the time when she'll be old enough to tackle some of the long-range cruising they plan in the Pacific.

These people, as I said, are all different, but they've all successfully adapted to boat life. The sea has turned them into democrats, and their liveaboard neighborhood stretches far beyond their dock, even to friends cruising in other parts of the world. Like homesteaders of another era, they have a sense of self-sufficiency, a closeness to nature and adventure. No house can be a magic carpet like their boat. Maybe that's why a house is always an "it" and a boat is always a "she." As one liveaboard told me, "You don't have to love a house to live there, but you do have to love a boat."

Could you do it? Sure. This book will give you answers to some of your questions. All you need is the dream.

Part I.
The Adjustments

1.

SELL THE WEDDING PRESENTS, BUY DRIP-DRY CLOTHES, TAKE A LAST DIP IN THE BATHTUB

Life on a boat is not like life in a house. That's precisely the reason people want to move aboard: It is more mobile, more adventuresome, closer to nature than life in a housing development or an apartment.

Naturally, it's a way of life that calls for changes in your expectations, depending on how much of an establishment life you've led. Obviously, a freewheeling young couple only a few years into the job market will probably have less difficulty than a couple in their forties with a large investment in a suburban life-style. But it can be done—even by establishment types. It was a couple in their forties, from a very straight background, who told me about their move onto a cutter in Newport Beach, California:

"Long before we made our decision, we would sit down, divide a sheet of paper into two columns, and list positive and negative considerations of moving on board. After living on the boat for a year, we reviewed our list. Oddly enough, many of the negatives have moved into the positive areas. Few negatives remain. Our plus side grows daily."

Certainly, you can list many reasons why you shouldn't live on a boat. There are things that will worry your parents, alien-

Dogs don't always have to stay behind. This poodle, Bonnie, lives on board a 44-foot sailboat.

ate your friends, break up a budding romance or even a marriage. We'd better talk about them because some people can live with them cheerfully—others can't.

We're not talking here about the problems of cruising overseas, wrestling with storms, and tinkering with broken-down engines. One of the big things we're talking about is as elementary as—space. You can get an idea of how much your space will shrink on a boat by chopping off rooms in your house or apartment until you are left with about the same linear dimensions as you'll have on your boat.

Let's say you can describe your apartment as having a length overall of 42 feet, a 30-foot beam, full standing room, and enough space for the flotsam and jetsam collected over the past five, ten, twenty, or more years: Art Deco sofas, ship models, areca palms, a few hundred books, and so forth. Trying to approximate your future boat may leave you standing in, say, a 9- by 12-foot bedroom, which is very roughly the space that one Florida couple and their son have on board the elderly 33-foot Alden-designed sloop they own. "We were living in a sixty- by twelve-foot mobile home," says the husband, who teaches school in St. Petersburg, "so we cut our living space drastically. We sold everything we owned except our clothes and some books. Hard? Oh, you really have to have your head together." Looking around the Alden, I realized there was little there that wasn't part of the boat when she was originally built in 1936—there simply isn't room. This loss of space (and the shrinkage is there even if you move to a 68-footer) is sort of the pivotal factor in moving aboard because it leads to some other restrictions.

De-possessionizing

There's a limit to space, so liveaboards retrench, simplify, reorder their lives. The closest analogy I can make is with backpacking. There, you carry on your back your galley, food, and spare gear. No nonessentials are allowed and the weight limit is on the order of 35 pounds. So it is when you move aboard.

It starts with subtraction—off-loading the books, the great posters you've had since college, the stuffed iguana. Then begins the rearguard action to keep the stuff off the boat, because possessions tend to multiply like wire coat hangers. Never again will you go to a country fair and bring home, with a clear conscience, a three-foot stuffed teddy bear. Instead, you may have to do what some unreconstructed liveaboards do and sit down once or twice a year to sort out and toss off anything not used in the past six months. Either that or cut in a new waterline!

The first step in moving aboard is usually a garage sale, which can be a time of anguish, pangs of regret, and even tears. If you're young, live in jeans anyway, and your wedding gifts ran to sleeping bags, not Doulton china, this isn't a hassle. For older people, it can be.

What goes? Any clothing that needs coddling or that can't be interchanged with the stuff next to it in the slim hanging locker. Collections you've had since childhood. Furniture you spent weekends refinishing. Most or all of the hanging plants.

The worst moment is when you make the initial decision, then it's easier, except for those few times during the garage sale when you spot a seedy-looking character fingering your Waterford crystal. Afterward, you'll feel cleansed. At least that's the way Sid Seddons put it. She's a comfortable, middle-class lady married to a fireman, and she made the transition to a Westsail 42 beautifully.

"I had a very liberated feeling after selling the possessions. It seemed strange to my sisters and parents that I could spend years collecting these things and get rid of them in a marathon two-week garage sale. What pleased me was that the kids got into the spirit of it right away. I told them that they had to get rid of some toys, so they brought them out. Then as the sale went on, they dragged out more toys. 'We ought to get rid of this stuff, too,' they told me."

Of course, it all doesn't have to go. Most liveaboards have a trunk or a garageful of belongings on land with their parents or friends, but they find even this slight umbilical cord becomes less important with time. One liveaboard puts it this way, "On a boat, you find you have enough storage for everything you need, except for stuff you don't use and never had the sense to throw away. We have a roomful of that kind of thing, and we barely look at it once a year. But it's 'good stuff' and we have to keep it."

What nonnecessities come aboard are few but more valued. I remember a tour of the 54-foot Burger *Lawtom* in Marathon, Florida. Bill and Paula Blevins who live on her pointed out that there were only three or four items on her that weren't utilitarian: a portrait of Mrs. Blevins's father, a poem framed in the galley, and some penguin figurines—memorabilia of Blevins's trips to Antarctica while in the navy. That, decided the Blevinses, was quite enough.

The Physically Smaller Universe

You can look at a boat in two ways when you're living aboard. If you're happy, love boats and the water, love the camaraderie of the dock, then you think of the boat as bigger than the confines of the hull. The living space spills over to the dock area, the pier, the whole harbor, in fact. "How can you say a boat is small?" asked a young woman aboard a 32-footer. "I've got the whole ocean." That's the attitude if you're happy.

You can learn to adapt, if you want to. A liveaboard on an Atkin double-ender ketch, told me: "You learn privacy tricks, such as turning your face outward while in your bunk or getting away in the forepeak."

If you're unhappy, the living space shrinks miserably until it seems smaller than the boundaries of the hull. Every knock to the shins, every stooping of the head, every banging of elbows while foraging in the bilges is an affront and a provocation. The unhappy liveaboard begins to feel like Alice in Wonderland trying to cope with normal-size teacups after she grew 30 feet tall.

There was a woman living on a boat, a very nice 36-foot sloop. She split. Why? The only way she could explain it was the main beam. She's tall, five feet seven, and the beam was about five feet four above the floorboards. She kept forgetting to duck (maybe, subconsciously, she wanted to get hit on the head; she was wobbly about living on board to start). Anyway, one particularly nasty knock on a particularly gray and drizzly day and she packed up her gear and left.

Living in the Lap of Each Other

If a boat can mean a lot of physical contact with table legs and boom, it also brings its share of perplexing human problems. You may know about the rat experiment—put enough of them in a small box and they start acting neurotic. A boat can become a box, and often enough it's the woman who finds it so. Perhaps because a boat usually begins as a man's toy, and the idea of moving on board may be his, not hers.

In Miami a few years ago, I ran across a liveaboard story that seemed to have fairy-tale beginnings. The usual handsome retired navy officer, a 48-foot trimaran, the inevitable pretty girl. All set to sail into the sunset. But the trimaran ended up on the salesblock and the man moved back on land to try to rekindle a romance that ended somewhere between a malfunctioning head and a group of curious strangers who wandered on board to "look at the pretty boat."

Certainly, the boat didn't look like a culprit. It had a main saloon big enough for a cocktail party and all the amenities, including a washer/drier. The man told me afterward, "People look on this life as romantic and terrific, but a white picket fence around a cottage, it's not. The trouble is, we were so close on the boat—it was like living in a small tent. To do it, you have to be on the best of terms and love boats, or you have problems." As we walked off the dock, he pointed out a white ketch that another bachelor was living on. "*His* girl friend loves the boat," he said rather wistfully. Proving that space is more a function of mind than matter.

You Never Thought You'd Miss _____.

It was a man living on a big ketch in Wisconsin who summed up best for me the problem liveaboards have with some of the small luxuries of life: "We not only live waterside, but we live quite simply. I have to say that the spirit is willing but the flesh has not yet completely gotten adjusted to basic amenities or their lack. So . . . a hot shower is a purification rite, making one reborn. An iced drink in summer is nectar, better than champagne. Plenty of ice to keep steak and greens fresh is very nice." You have to give up some things that fall loosely into a category we could call "life-style." Some of the small pleasures of life. These are a few of the gaps suggested by liveaboards I talked to.

"*A good reference library*," said a retired professor. "I miss up-to-date knowledge of what's going on in geology and related fields." We might add museums and university facilities to the list if you're cruising or living in a remote coastal area.

"*The beautiful convenience of my own hot shower*," said a woman on a 27-foot cutter in Hawaii: "The harbor shower facilities are really inadequate. Two showers for about one hundred fifty liveaboard women, with a twenty-five-gallon hot-water tank. It's a major inconvenience." And a lot of other live-aboards miss a bathtub, though a charming Austrian woman on a trimaran in the Keys admitted to me, "I never even liked bathtubs before I moved on board."

Bookshelves. For library-size books as well as paperbacks. There's never enough room.

Washers and driers. You come into port after a long wet thrash and wet clothing is piled high below. What's the last thing you want to do? Go to a laundromat. It's a hassle for almost every liveaboard save the few fortunate (let's add well-to-do) ones who have on-board facilities.

Ice cubes. As many as you want. Many liveaboards have limited or no freezer capacity. Of course, if you're cruising full time, the situation gets more drastic. Who wants to pay $4 for 15 pounds of ice in the Bahamas?

Flush toilets that don't need an afterthought. Pumping heads gets to some people, and everyone hates holding tanks, where raw sewage is stored until it can be emptied out at a dumping station ("Frankly, it makes boating stink," says one outspoken lady). Alternatives: the luxury of an electric head, which eliminates the pumping, or the marina restrooms, which eliminate some strain on the holding tank. (But as one Hawaii liveaboard says, "Some mornings, the run to the john is god-awful.")

A *cozy fireplace.* You can have one on a boat, of course, but it brings up the problems of getting and storing wood.

Openness. Jim Hostetter lives with his family on a Challenger 40 in California. What would he like? "Windows to really view the outside: rainstorms, boats, people, happenings in the bay."

And because he travels a lot as an airline pilot: "Room to unpack after a two-week trip."

Easy communications. Unless you have a phone on board, just making a telephone call can be a real hassle, even if it's only the inconvenience of a two-block walk.

A garage. For the car, if you need one, and for extra tools if you're a handyman.

Grass under your toes. Some people really miss their garden. A comfortable solution is to bring some plants with you or do as Esther Bradley did in St. Petersburg. She "adopted" a 1,500-foot-long strip of land bordering the fence around the municipal marina and turned the parched strip into a garden full of flowering plants and cacti. It's just a few steps from the Chris-Craft Cavalier 35 on which she lives.

Finally, most subtle point of all, "A floor that doesn't move." That's the suggestion of John Hauser who lives on a Pearson 26 in California.

There Are Some Failures

When I asked a number of happy liveaboards why some of their acquaintances had given up and moved ashore, here were some of the responses:

"I'd say the failure rate is about seventy-five percent. Major causes are small children who are unhappy, small living space, no knowledge of boats, and a wife or husband who has no interest in boating."

"The two biggest causes for 'grief' seem to be inability to cope and an unrealistic appraisal of the costs involved with no allowance for emergencies."

"Cramped quarters, dampness, inadequate heat, lack of adequate bathing facilities. I'd put the failure rate at eighty-five percent."

"Failures? The only one I know of moved ashore to a nursing home in his eighties when he was very feeble."

"I don't know how many fail, but most of the people I have

known in the past ten years of living aboard buy the wrong boat. Usually, it's too small and the everyday facts of living become difficult: the wife cooking on a hot plate, no refrigeration, no headroom, no privacy for babies. I've met wives who wanted a lot of gewgaws they couldn't have aboard, and one fellow who wanted to have a kind of social life that wasn't suited for his too small boat."

"I'd say about twenty-five percent return to land because they can't adjust to confinement and lack of privacy. Or they miss conveniences like dishwashers, washing machines, garbage disposals, and the rest."

"Failure rate here [Florida] is about seventy-five percent I'd guess. Lack of space for 'things.' Discomfort of ocean passages. Lack of income because marinas are expensive and most people want to live at a dock. No room for children. Not having a total commitment to the idea from the start. These are all reasons for failure."

"We place the liveaboard failure rate at eighty percent. Major causes seem to be poor planning, poor finances, and the inability to understand the fact that living aboard is a different way of life, not merely an ongoing vacation from reality."

"Too many front-end compromises. If you want to live a 'straight life' five days a week, they better be comfortable days and nights."

"You need to be a well-balanced 'whole' person, content within yourself. You can't feel the need or importance to have every item in a full-page newspaper ad. You have to be content to listen to the birds, watch a pretty sunset, and wave at a friend sailing past."

Amen.

2.

CAN YOU MAKE A LIVING DOING THIS?

Late afternoon, the bottle of burgundy emptying slowly, a barometer of how well the conversation is going. We were sitting in the cabin of *Hawkeye,* an elderly cruiser built by Hodgdon Brothers in Maine about 40 years ago. We being myself and *Hawkeye's* owners, Jim and Kelli Boothman. The Boothmans make their living partly by chartering *Hawkeye.* It's not an unusual way of life. Visit an anchorage like this one off Dinner Key Marina in Miami and you find yourself in the middle of a cottage industry where the itinerant way of life has to be supported by your wits and hard labor. People who live on the hook get a little tired of being called "boat bums" so the conversation quickly got around to the rebuttal. Immediate topic: a black-hulled sloop being motored past by a suntanned young woman in her twenties.

"There goes Evelyn," said Jim. "She used to run a sail loft in the Islands. Worked for a sailmaker here for a while, but she said she couldn't stand the static. Very independent. I saw her shoveling dirt last week for a garden at Dinner Key. They stored her sails and she was working the payment off."

"And they say we're bums," Kelli interrupted. "We have to work harder when we're living on the hook than those people in the marina. Just getting our water out here is hard work."

Do I want proof? She's got it. There's the woman on that white-hulled ketch who makes cabin curtains and upholsters bunk pads on board. There's the fellow over there who makes $3 an hour varnishing and painting the fat-cat boats in the marina—"You can't get jobs like that out here in the anchorage. We do our own work." There's the woman who sews cotton duck workpants with anchors appliquéd on the pockets. A pair climbs aboard at that moment, worn by David, former electrical engineer from Arkansas, who's rowed over from a ferrocement ketch. After modeling the home-sewn (sloop-sewn?) pants, David tells me that he and his shipmate also pick up odd jobs on land. At the moment, he's a busboy and she's a waitress at a restaurant in Coconut Grove. The only drawback to the jobs, he confides, is that you can get hung up on money. Right now he wants to cut out for the Islands for six months, but his mate is into building up a nest egg.

Compared to David and some of the others in the anchorage, Jim and Kelli seem almost suburban. Settled. But talk to them and you get the feeling that theirs was the more extreme break with the past, the more unexpected decision. After all, they dropped out, so to speak, in their late forties at a time when Kelli was working for an art journal and Jim was running a photography studio in Old Saybrook, Connecticut. It was just after he won some awards in a Connecticut professional exhibit that he got an offer to buy his studio and he and Kelli decided, as easily as a nod, to take it.

They bought a 50-foot Chris-Craft and moved on board, only to fall into the transitional trap of a lot of liveaboards: They tried to treat their boat like a house. No good. They hit the marketplace again and this time purchased a boat that couldn't be treated like a house, a classic Hand-design outfitted and ready for long-range cruising. *Hawkeye,* as they named her, has suited them just fine.

Realistically, the Boothmans know that their boat doesn't have the kind of fancy trimmings to make it a floating pleasure palace, the kind that's competitive in the charter trade. This puts some restrictions on them because they can't run their charter rates too high. They ask $400 a week, $300 for midweek, $150 for a weekend, and $75 a day. This is for one couple—all *Hawkeye* can handle besides the Boothmans—and includes three meals a day with wine at dinner, use of the dinghy, fishing tackle, and snorkeling gear. Liquor and special menus (steak and lobster) are extra. So are marina charges if the charterer wants to tie up instead of hooking it.

Occasional chartering won't make them rich, but the Boothmans figure that 8 to 15 weeks of it a year give them enough to live on. Best of all, it pays them to do what they like best— cruise. *Hawkeye* has been spending summers at Fishers Island in the north, winters at Dinner Key.

There are liabilities. Charterers can notoriously be rough on a boat, even with the owners/crew watching over them. ("Next ad we run," says Kelli, "I'm going to put in that you must have an old pair of boat shoes.") There was the fellow who left the switch of the electric head turned to "on" and burned it out. His wife had to use a bucket for three days and was so constipated, the Boothmans had to take her finally to a marina.

Then there was the little guy who came on board with the big blonde he insisted was his wife. He was a genuinely likable guy, but he got in his cups at night and would accidentally kick in a screen or fall in the drink. Otherwise, he would stay in the aft cabin with the blonde and the Boothmans would wander discreetly forward. You do, they admit, lose a certain amount of your freedom when you charter.

You also have to like to cook. Kelli does, fortunately, and willingly turns out French toast at seven and stellar buffets at noon and night. If you can't hack making London broil after a day of working a boat, chartering can definitely be a drag. No one else is going to do it, least of all the charterer who expects a certain amount of coddling.

Nor can you rely on the charterer to help with a boat. Fortunately, *Hawkeye* can easily be handled by the Boothmans. They did make the mistake once of asking a fellow to take the stern line. He did. He picked it up and jumped on land with it. There he stood on the dock while the Boothmans in dismay watched the boat's stern swing gently out into the channel.

The Boothmans turned to chartering to supplement their income because their photography business didn't transfer as successfully as they hoped it would from land to sea. When they moved aboard five years ago, Jim planned to continue photographing hot racing boats and selling prints to the owners. He had been doing this successfully on Long Island Sound, sometimes earning as much as a couple of thousand dollars in a big race.

He and Kelli figured they could do the same thing on the racing circuit in Florida. What they learned when they started cruising was that this kind of business depended a great deal on permanent land contacts. If you were to bump into the boat owners at parties before the race, you were apt to sell them your photos. In the South, Jim lost this personal contact and only a couple of his photos were picked up, though a number of the slides he sent out on approval were kept and probably used by owners who didn't know him and figured they weren't likely to meet him. Annoying? Yes, but that's one of the liabilities of cruising and making a living.

After five years on their boat, Jim and Kelli are tough realists and they have two firm pieces of advice for anyone who hopes to make a living on board.

First, get the boat paid off before you skip land. Whether you build it yourself, refurbish an old boat, or have a mortgage on a new one, get all the bills settled while you have a steady income on land. Nothing is more depressing than facing a future with uncertain income levels and fixed bank interest charges to pay every month.

Second, have at least a couple of thousand dollars on hand to tide you over the first year. And treat it with respect. "When we first moved on board," says Kelli, "we thought our savings would last forever. We knew we couldn't live on nothing, but we learned you need more than the cost of food. The boat will need work and the repair bills can be pretty heavy if you're trying to live on forty or fifty dollars a week." She tells a story about how she and Jim decided to have dinner at a pretty good restaurant the month before. The bill came to about $30 and blew their budget out of kilter for the rest of the month. "How come our money isn't lasting this month?" wondered Jim. "Because we ate out!" Kelli reminded him.

A Transition That Worked:
At Sea in an Art Gallery

Viken is a 35-foot Ericson, vintage 1967; she's also a roving gallery-cum-studio for her two artist owners, David and Zora Aiken. The day I met the Aikens, they were flopped out in the cockpit, enjoying a balmy 80-degree February day at Duck Key in the Florida Keys. Now you might be tempted to think that the Aikens are really having a good time of it, but after a little conversation, you find they're working. Not only do they both paint and draw on *Viken*, but they use her to nudge their way into little fishing ports up and down the East Coast and Canada to find subjects to draw. When they're sitting, they're usually observing and there's often a sketchpad at hand.

They're a handsome couple, in their mid-thirties, and you can imagine them fitting into the Chicago advertising/art world they were part of for ten years when David worked as an art director for a large advertising agency and Zora was developing her style in oils (she's a graduate of the Chicago Art Institute). Then they did something a bit perplexing to their parents. They decided to move on board their Ericson 27 for a summer to see if they could hack that way of life. They could. Later they bought their present 35-footer, went south to the Keys and north to Canada in the summer, and started painting in earnest. Their parents are now reconciled, incidentally: "Now that they can see the results and know we really are working and not fooling around."

It's gratifying to David and Zora that after just two and one-half years of living aboard, they can make a living doing the kind of work they want to do. As a backup, they did take the precaution of getting a license to charter but they haven't had to do it so far. During the first year, David says they had to do some advertising sketches and other bits and pieces to help pay the bills, but no longer. The secret, besides being talented, is setting up land contacts with gallery owners they knew before leaving and honoring their commitments as firmly as they would were they on land. And, "Fortunately," adds Zora, "we have a diversity of mediums. When we exhibit, people think we're a *group*."

Before leaving Chicago, the Aikens made sure they could get through at least a year without financial stress. "We thought there might be problems," says David, "and there were. For one thing, I said I would work in a gas station if I had to to support us. Wouldn't you know—that was the year of the gas shortage!" So they counted on their $5,000 in savings to get started, but only had to fall back on $3,000 of it. David also suggests: "Get all your bills paid before you leave. Don't go with boat payments. And *know how to sail*. Otherwise, you can end up like a couple we knew who tried to do this and had to fall back on unemployment."

David modified the Ericson to give Zora and himself more room to work and store their art supplies. He changed the cabin arrangement from a dinette to a standard two-pilot-berth with a fold-up table. He also turned a quarter berth into a chart table and put shelves in a hanging locker for more usable space. The one drawback to *Viken* is that they haven't been able to keep a few favorite paintings ("Fortunately, friends bought them"); their on-board gallery is restricted to a couple of small drawings.

As far as working space goes, however, *Viken* is more than adequate. David likes to work on deck, which is suitable for his mediums—he does watercolors, ink sketches, and woodcuts. Zora found that she had to work below, as she works in oil and couldn't keep the dust and flies outside off her canvases—she's often wondered how old-time landscape artists did it. So she uses the forward cabin, propping her canvases up on the portable easel resting on the V-berths and keeping the area ventilated by opening the overhead hatch.

"When I start doing oils, we have to *sit*," she tells me. That's another occupational problem because oils require sufficient drying time, so Zora has started working with acrylics, which aren't so opaque and require a different approach, but have the practical advantage of drying almost immediately. Transferring a studio to a boat, Zora has found, requires a bit of translation—some modification—as well as hard work.

She and David both feel the boat has opened them up to a world of subject matter they couldn't reach in a Chicago apartment. *Viken* has taken them to the Marquesas, to Sanibel, to out-of-the-way fishing villages like Bon Secour, Alabama, where they went Christmas caroling with fishermen last December and ended up serenading the prisoners in the town jail from the top of a flatbed trailer. They've wandered through the Keys— David is working on a book about cruising that he is writing and illustrating—as well as up to Canada, and they're thinking of the canals of France in a couple of years.

Along the way, they've met other people doing pretty much the same thing: using their talents to make a living on board. There was the children's book author who had raised two children while living on board for the past 28 years. The wood craftsman who works his way from port to port: "His own boat is his calling card." The fellow on a small power cruiser who carries his sandblasting gear on board and picks up assignments in boatyards as he cruises. The occupations differ, but the results are the same. As David says, "It's like having an employer who gives you fifty-two weeks of vacation a year."

A Primer for Roving Craftsmen

A prime concern of people who want to cruise is whether or not they can make a living by picking up odd jobs in ports here and abroad. I spoke to a few people who've done this and found that it is possible. What's marketable? We've mentioned a few things already (sandblasting, sewing on board) and the fact is that with some imagination almost any skill can be turned to cash. For instance, there was the young woman who sold home-baked bread to other boats in her anchorage in the Virgins. Midmorning, she would hop into her dinghy and row from boat to boat until the morning's baking was gone. And while she was at it, she took orders for home-baked pies and cakes. Obviously, this kind of business, netting about $40 a week, won't support a family, but it can keep the cash flowing in.

Probably your best bet, especially overseas where you can get into hassles about work permits, is to acquire and market repairs on engines and electronic gear. Things are always breaking down on boats. Good mechanics are always hard to come by. Maybe the best investment you can make in your voyage before you leave is to equip your boat with a good workshop. On one boat I saw, the port V-berth in the forward cabin had been raised to counter height, strongly reinforced, and turned into a workbench, complete with vise, a good assortment of hand tools mounted on the bulkhead, and, most important, storage below for a good stock of spare engine parts.

As for prospects, here is what three world cruisers told me quite honestly. (Among them, they've sailed to over 50 foreign countries on five continents.)

Said one, "Very speculative unless you're a shipwright, rigger, or skilled mechanic."

The second: "Southern Spain and the West Indies are without trained personnel, like mechanics, radio and electronics engineers. But permits to work legally are nearly unobtainable. However, it's done and they're paid under the table. As for girls: rich, poor, clean, dirty, fair, or ugly—they can get crewing jobs rather easily, though how they are paid or how much they are paid is unknown to me. The boat owner above all wants to be sure there won't be any seasickness and that they can cook."

And the third told me: "If you are a welder or a pharmacist with OK papers, you can get work anywhere. Otherwise, you're competing in the local unskilled job market. Personally, I think it's better to borrow and pay back a few years later when you return to the U.S. wage scale. I will say that you can always earn a few dollars by being willing to do what someone wants done for what he is willing to pay."

A man who has traded his boatyard skills—he's a fairly able woodworker but will try anything—offered this advice. First and most important, he says, is to make yourself seen. You won't find work sitting in the boat. Go to pubs and restaurants near the harbor where you're likely to run into boat owners or crew-members. Find out who needs work done.

Next, turn yourself into a local. This has to do with being seen—if you look familiar to people, they're more apt to listen when you ask for work. A nice trick is to give yourself an air of permanence and respectability with business cards. Seriously. Have a bunch printed up by the neighborhood printer before you leave: your name, the boat's name, and a line about what you can do ("engine repairs," "photographer," "loving care for boats," "handyman *extraordinaire*"—whatever). Leave space to write in where you can be reached locally: a slip number, name of anchorage, place where a phone number can be left.

Now, if you're walking around soft-selling your abilities to the fellows in the local pub (incidentally, bartenders are great sources of odd jobs), you're already advertising. Do some more. Put a sign in your rigging. Put up a little note on the bulletin board at the local yard, pub, or even yacht club—with your business card attached, it looks professional.

Ask for referrals. "People seem to be hesitant about hiring us," says one liveaboard in Kailua, Hawaii. "Comes from the old stereotypes of 'hippie' and 'vagabond.' But competency at work convinces them otherwise." If you've done a good job for one boat owner, ask if he has friends. It doesn't hurt to get a letter of recommendation that might be useful in your next port. Incidentally, another fellow who's cruised around the world says to cultivate Americans. Many countries require work permits, but you can often avoid legal problems, he says, by working on a foreign yacht—for example, an American yacht stopping in a French port.

Finally and most important, don't categorize yourself too closely. If things are tight, go knock on doors in American ports. Drive a taxi. Or pick blueberries for farmers. One fellow hopped out of his French port to pick grapes in the Bordeaux country—not much money, but he got room, board, and all the wine he could drink.

You may sometimes pick up a job offer, like the vineyard work, that means leaving the boat. Don't do it unless you know a local or have friends or family on board to watch the vessel. And do be prepared to go if it means some money. Yacht delivery jobs can sometimes materialize as long as you don't mind leaving your friends or family temporarily, and if delivery captains or owners find you responsible and available, this sort of thing crops up more often.

DON'T COUNT ON CHARTERING FOR A PENNY. It's very tempting, but if you're planning to do any serious cruising, you won't have the permanence necessary to establish yourself and advertise. Chartering is a cutthroat business at best, highly competitive and with small margins of profit unless you do it regularly. You also need to pamper the guests, chat with them nonstop, answer all their questions, entertain them, and keep them in comfort. All of which means having a glamorous boat that's in the $100,000 range, scuba equipment, fancy Avon dinghy, and all the rest. Even a couple like the Boothmans who only look for a few weeks of it a year will admit it's a tough trade to get into.

If you do have a good, clean boat, however, and get friendly with the manager of a resort hotel, especially in outlying areas, he may come up with some day charters. One cruising couple, for instance, got into a conversation with a fellow on the docks of the San Juan Yacht Club. They had just come in for a week's stay and discovered that this fellow and his wife had been all over the island trying to find a boat that would take them out for some really serious sailing. The cruising couple agreed on the spot to spend a day out with them for $60. "Apparently, there was a small charter fleet in the harbor," the man told me, "but this fellow and his wife wanted to handle the boat themselves and the charter captain wouldn't agree. I figured I could take over if he and his wife proved inept, but they were damn good sailors and they brought along a bottle of rum and a couple bottles of wine to boot."

3.

GROWING UP ON A BOAT:
HOW MANY CHILDREN DO YOU KNOW
WHO'VE SWUM WITH A PORPOISE?

Janice Marois is slender and stands just about five feet tall, which is a happy accident of nature, because for 18 of her 19 years, from the time she was born until just about a year ago, she lived on her parents' 40-foot cruiser *Butch*. As she puts it, *Butch* is pretty comfortable for two, but a little cramped for three, so it's just as well she didn't take up a lot of space.

When I met Janice, she was working for the Chamber of Commerce of Marathon in the Florida Keys and missing life on the boat. Why did she move off at 18? "Well, it was this *job*. You see I got it the summer I graduated and I stayed on the boat at first. But we like to go cruising on weekends. Well, sometimes I'd be late for work. Actually I *was* on time, but a day or two late. You see, we'd be out cruising and the weather would turn nasty, so I'd wake up at eight on Monday morning and we'd still be two hundred miles out of Marathon. What can you do?" She moved on land—tentatively.

"You can see I still wear deck shoes. That's the only kind of shoes I owned until New Year's Eve. I got a job for the night as a cocktail waitress at the Indies Inn and I had to buy a pair of sandals. I just couldn't wear deck shoes with the long dress, could I?"

Janice was fated to live on a boat long before she saw daylight. The plans for *Butch* were her father's first anniversary present to her mother. He built the boat himself and when Janice was born, she went straight into a nursery netted off in the forward cabin.

When she was growing up on a boat in the fifties, living aboard was an uncommon life-style and people's reactions went two ways. When she was in kindergarten, a classmate had a birthday party and everyone was invited except Janice; the boy's parents figured she must be rich to live on a "yacht" (landlubbers get a little inexact) and wouldn't enjoy a simple little party. The more usual reaction was that she and her folks were boat bums or floating gypsies. Fortunately, her parents are cheerful, philosophic people and taught her to be happy with the friends she did make on land and at the marinas and anchorages.

One of the great advantages of boat life for Janice was that she could make two different sets of friends. Because boats are a great equalizer, the friends she made on the dock came in all sizes, shapes, and ages. As she says, she spent a lot of time in the Keys on the same pier as a well-known surgeon and the head of the math department at the University of Florida. So "Professor B—— and Dr. H—— would tell me anything I needed to know about math and science." Which must have been successful because she generally made A's in school.

As for children her own age, usually there was at least one living on a boat wherever her parents took her. "When I was about four and we were in Daytona, there were no kids in the marina, but that was OK because there were the ducks. Mallards. We started out with a few pairs and they bred and pretty soon we had ninety-one. I fed them and gave them all names, even the Canadian goose, Nasty Nasser, who joined them after a while."

Often, too, there were cruising families passing through, and when they found there was a child living in the marina, they'd stay a day or two longer so she could meet their kids. Sometimes, months later, Janice would get a letter postmarked the

Marquesas or the Azores, but she learned very young that not everyone who said he was going around the world did it. "The ones who talked the most about it seemed to be the ones who never got farther than Key West. It was the ones who were very quiet, didn't talk about the future, who'd quietly leave one morning and do it."

The one thing her shore friends never understood was how Janice could live in the small cabin she had on *Butch*. Actually, she probably had more room than a lot of boat kids who sometimes share a cabin or make do with just a berth. Janice never found her quarters too small, simply because she had different standards. She figured the land kids had a big room filled with junk they never used, while she had a small room full of things she needed. And she probably had as much stowage space for the necessities of life as kids living in houses; they had more drawers and closets, but a lot of these were filled with stuff rarely used or outgrown. "I had a locker for my shoes, a closet for dresses, a bin for my flippers and diving mask, a bookshelf. My father even fit two stereo speakers in at either end of the bookshelf."

Growing up on a boat gave Janice an appreciation of space that few land children can learn. "How many times do you really use a dining room in a house?" she asked. "When my parents wanted to have a big sit-down dinner for Christmas last year, we found the space. We put the table in the cockpit and led it through the doors into the main saloon and we had sixteen at it. We use the space we have and we don't have big empty rooms sitting around doing nothing."

Janice says that it is true that boat children sometimes have problems adjusting to land after prolonged cruising while they're young. I had heard of a baby who learned to walk on a boat where he spent about 90 percent of his time. When his mother started taking him on land with her, he had to actually learn how to walk again on a nonmoving platform. Janice had her own story. When she was three years old, her parents bought her a tricycle. She rode it around and around the cockpit of their boat, then made a trial run on land where she continued making tight little circles. Her mother patiently explained it was possible to go in a straight line on land.

Naturally, boat life had some drawbacks, though Janice feels they're pretty minor ones. "It was a struggle with just one head when I got to the stage where I was interested in makeup. Finally, my father just gave up and got me a big makeup mirror for my cabin so I wouldn't tie the head up all evening.

"Also, Mom wouldn't let me have a dog. Turtles, OK, but no dogs. We did a lot of anchoring out and she knew me pretty well. I just wouldn't be the type of person who'd row in every time the dog needed to go."

Small points, really, and far outweighed by the good ones. Catching a baby hammerhead with her fishing rod when she was five. Swimming with a porpoise at an anchorage ("When I climbed back on the boat, he stayed around the stern for a few hours, waiting for me to come back and play"). Diving in the coral reefs off the Keys. Getting out of school at noon on a Friday and taking off with her parents on a fishing trip. Circulating letters among a group of a dozen or so cruising live-aboard children.

Does she want to move back? You bet. If she marries, he'll have to love boats and want to live on one. "Boats are great. If you don't like the neighbors, you can move. And getting dressed up means putting on deck shoes. Ties? They're for landlubbers."

Will They Get Sick? Will They Need More Privacy? How About Schools?

Janice's experiences are fairly typical of cruising children. It's a way of life that seems to foster self-reliance, imagination, and health. But there are some adjustments that parents have to make, especially with very young children.

Infants

Children rely on their parents on land for their well-being, and even more so on a boat, which is an unpredictable platform, buffeted by wind and water.

People have made ocean voyages with infants, but it's not an everyday occurrence and it shouldn't be. It means making judicious decisions concerning routes, with alternative destinations in case of emergency, and seasons, and possibly having these decisions wrecked by storms or lack of wind. It means the psychological risk of being far from land and worrying about the infant getting ill. And it means choosing a crew with extreme care. Babies don't stop crying because they're at sea, and their human demands can be destructive when crewmembers are coming off watch dead tired. I only know a handful of people who've done long cruises with infants, and in all cases they were extremely able seamen; in several cases, the mother or father had medical training.

World cruising isn't recommended before a child is at least two or three. Even then, the benefit to the child is not great. Five- and six-year-olds are just barely able to remember some of the details of their cruises in later years; an infant has all the inconveniences and none of the memories.

Whether you're cruising or staying put, your boat will need modification for a child. Teri and Gary Foulger of Newport Beach, California, for instance, heavily modified their 42-footer *Wind Borne* for daughter Skye Blue who was born on board with the help of a doctor and a midwife (*Wind Borne* motored over to the doctor's own dock at the right time, and just a few hours after Skye arrived, the boat was heading back to her own marina). Gary was careful to make sure Skye would have support on deck and below on the shifting platform of her new home. He devised a kind of sling that could be fastened to the boom on deck or to the overhead beams in the cabin. These support ropes attached to Skye's halter and kept her upright when she moved about.

A sturdy, well-padded crib is a must. It doesn't have to be fancy. You can build it of plywood or simply wedge an oversize rubber clothes basket between bunks. An inventive California couple made a high-sided macrame bassinet that swings with the motion of the boat.

Under way, cruising couples generally recommend keeping

young children on safety harnesses. (It goes without saying that lifelines are not enough when a child is on board; also put up a mesh material around the whole inner perimeter.) On deck, add a simple, well-padded swimming vest, which will provide flotation and also buffer the child on rough days when he might be more likely to fall or bump into things. A good safety vest is made by Stearns Manufacturing (St. Cloud, Minnesota 56301). It's called the Kindergåård and it's designed for toddlers weighing under 50 pounds. There's a lot of flotation around the head so the child will be turned face up in the water in a matter of seconds. The problem with ordinary vests is that they usually don't support the heavy head sufficiently when the child hits the water.

If you plan to cruise with a toddler, keep him off commercial baby foods right from the start. Natural foods are better for him than the sugar-dosed pap sold on grocery store shelves, and the commercial baby foods just aren't available off the beaten track. One cruising mother strongly advises breast-feeding; milk supplies overseas are notoriously uneven in quality, and sterilizing bottles on a pitching cruiser is an exercise in masochism.

We mentioned the problem of a child crying on long voyages. This is a real nuisance in packed marinas where a liveaboard can disturb neighbors who would otherwise be friendly. Dockmasters are actually more alive to the disturbance than other liveaboards who mostly tend to be understanding. One California family had to move twice because the dockmasters got uptight about the baby.

A supply of disposable diapers is a must because handling diapers stinks, literally, the way marine heads are set up these days; but then so does just going to the head yourself. Under way, although outboard discharge laws prohibit it, some mothers just bundle the diapers in a plastic mesh bag and drag them behind until clean. A woman who cruised the Islands doing this said the only disadvantage is that the diapers get very salty. Rinse them in fresh water, if you can, and keep the child's bottom well powdered and dry.

School-Age Children

The big requirement here is privacy, the more the better. Children can sometimes get by, temperamentally, with a bunk, but a cabin for themselves is better. Best is having it separated from the parents' cabin by the saloon. One fellow who ended up divorced after a year and a half of cruising told me bluntly, "Frankly, our sex life went to hell with the two kids on the other side of a curtain."

None of the cruising parents I spoke to keep children this age in lifejackets, unless under way in heavy weather. However, their boats were all "fenced" with double lifelines and mesh, just as useful for protecting adults aboard in rough weather as children.

A good reference to have on hand, not only for care of children but for adults as well, is *Advanced First Aid Afloat,* by Peter F. Eastman, M.D., a physician who's also a boatman. It tells you what to do if a stove flare-up burns the cook, or your child starts to hallucinate—just about everything from handling near-drowning to heat exhaustion. The language is blessedly nontechnical.

As far as toys and red wagons go, kids seem adept at working out their own substitutions—a dinghy instead of a bicycle, a shell collection instead of toy soldiers. Most liveaboards reported that their children had no problems giving up all the trappings of land life and proved to be perfectly happy fashioning their own toys out of driftwood and scraps.

You do get a partial confrontation with land life versus your life when the kids are enrolled in school. The old prejudices against "boat bums" have pretty much disappeared, especially in cities like St. Petersburg and Fort Lauderdale where there are sizable liveaboard populations. But I did hear reports of kids being hassled by some of their classmates and even a few teachers.

A family living on a Westsail in Newport Beach gave me an-

other slant on the school problem. It seems they had been dis-
cussing for some time the long cruise to the South Pacific they
would make when the kids were a couple of years older. One
day, the nine-year-old came home from school and wanted to
know what would happen "when we get caught in a big storm."
He was obviously troubled and his mother, after asking some
questions, found that the kids at school and his teacher had
been asking him that question, not in a malicious way, but out
of curiosity. "I just took him aside quietly," his mother told me,
"and explained that Dad and I both hoped that wouldn't
happen, but if it did, we knew what had to be done. Then I
explained what we would do in a very matter-of-fact way that
seemed to reassure him. He's only nine, of course, and I was
worried that he'd have recurring fears, but he didn't. Maybe
because I seemed calm about the prospect. He forgot about
the whole thing."

Another family, in San Francisco, faced a similar situation
when their daughter's teacher wanted to know about medical
care on the Pacific cruise they were planning. They explained
to her that they had a well-stocked medicine cabinet on board
and had spent a day with a doctor friend learning how to ob-
serve an ill child and relay information about her condition
over the radio to a physician who would advise them on proper
treatment for her. "The one thing this episode taught us," says
the father, "is that teachers and kids can throw a lot of fear into
a child if they don't sail themselves and don't understand the
preparations that go into a well-planned voyage. We spent
some time with the teacher. She was a young girl who had
never been involved with boats, and I think she was pretty
surprised to find out we weren't half-baked adventurers who
were dragging our kids off to a life of scurvy and drugs. My
wife capped it off by sending her some home-baked bread from
our galley."

Another cruising couple, very experienced, say you should
make a point of meeting land-based teachers "the way you
would customs officials in a newly emerged nation—with shined

shoes, tie, and good manners. They may not have said so to the kids, but they probably think you're crazy living on a boat."

Cruising people have known for years that there's an alternative to the land school system. If you see a boat motoring down the Intracoastal or on the hook in St. Thomas with the kids on deck with their schoolbooks and Mom wielding the red pencil, you've probably come face-to-face with a floating classroom run by the Calvert School. The Calvert Day School in Baltimore, Maryland, started a Home Instruction Division 60 years ago for the children of missionaries and State Department officials overseas who couldn't educate their children in the local schools. Today, about 3,000 children a year study with the Calvert system, including kids with circus troops, with parents in the military, and with overseas missions.

Cruising parents who have used the system admit they felt some trepidation about trying to tutor their own children and keeping their interest. They needn't have worried. To a man, they reported the kids enjoyed the lessons, made rapid progress, and picked up a lot of local color they would have missed in a conventional schoolroom. "Imagine," says one mother, "the impact of studying world history in Hong Kong Harbor."

William W. Kirk, headmaster of Calvert, told me that the school has courses in kindergarten (a new one for kids of four and five) through eighth grade. Each course is based on the regular day-school curriculum of the Calvert School in Baltimore, which serves as a kind of laboratory for the home courses. Parents don't need teaching experience, he stressed, because a special manual with detailed instructions is supplied. (On pp. 32–38 are excerpts from the first-grade manual and the sixth-grade manual so you can see how complete these instructions are—very reassuring!)

For the benefit of cruising parents, he pointed out that the courses are not designed for second-term enrollments. If you plan to begin a cruise at midyear, it's best to tutor the child at home for the fall term so you can follow through easily. Courses are set up to follow the regular nine-month school year (with

FIRST GRADE   *LESSON 17*

> I wouldn't stay there
>   Giving nobody joy;
> I'd fall down at once
>   And say, "Eat me, my boy!"

GAMES AND ACTIVITIES: With your pupil very near you and hiding his eyes say:

> I am very tall. (1)
> Now I am very small. (2)
> Sometimes I am tall. (1)
> Sometimes I am small. (2)
> Guess what I am now? (3)

(1) Stand on your toes and reach up. (2) Stoop. (3) Either stay in a stooping position or stand on your toes.

The child tries to guess your position before opening his eyes. Repeat, changing places with your pupil.

LESSON 18

ARITHMETIC: Draw on the plain pad a set whose members are a $\triangle$, a $\bigcirc$, and a $\square$. Tell the pupil that he can choose but one of these figures. Say: Let us see how many choices we have when we pick only one of the figures. Then show the choices as follows.

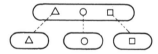

Repeat the activity with the stipulation that the pupil can choose any two figures at a time. This should result in the following drawing.

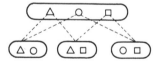

These same activities can be done with a set of three objects or a set of three toys.

Mathematics worktext, page 21. Relate panel 1 to the prebook activities by having your pupil form subsets of 2 each from a set of 3 objects.

Have the pupil separate a set of 4 objects to discover different subsets of 3 members each.

If he requires additional help, use a set of four real objects and select subsets having two objects each.

Use a procedure similar to that in the prebook activities to help the pupil discover the number of subsets of 3 objects each that can be made from a set of 4 objects.

Continue the activities with a set of four objects to find all possible subsets (no objects, 1 object, 2 objects, 3 objects, 4 objects).

The idea of subset (set within a set) is basic for many applications to daily life (classrooms in a school building) and for a meaningful grasp of the operations on numbers.

The number of possible subsets that can be formed from a given set of objects is fixed for that set and depends only on its cardinal number. We consider the empty set and the set itself as possible subsets of any set.

READING: Give your child his copy of the pre-primer, *Sun Up.* Tell him that the words on the cover tell the *title* of the book, and the *title* is the name of the book. Let him read it aloud. . . .

As he turns to the first page, tell him this is called the title page. Let him read the title here, then turn to the next two pages and say: "We call these pages the *Contents.* The Contents tells the titles of the stories and the pages on which each begins. The word at the top of the page says *Stories,* and under it are all the titles of the stories in the book." Point to the title of the first story, and the page on which it begins.

As the child turns to p. 5, lead him to discover that pp. 4 and 5 make up one illustration.

Directed Reading: Give your child a marker to hold under each line in order to discourage "finger pointing." . . .

Always encourage discussion of the story, both as to illustrations and ideas.

Skill Building: Review initial sounds by displaying the word cards for *Bing, Sandy,* and *was,* asking your child to name other words that begin with the same sound.

Print these words and sentences on a sheet of paper:

> The sun was up.
> Bing and Sandy
> Sandy was up.
> Sun Up

Have your child read each line silently and tell whether it is a sentence. He should note the capital letter that begins each sentence and the period that ends it.

Use those same words and sentences in this way: Point to a line and tell the pupil to arrange his word cards so they say the same thing. Have him read it aloud. You may now wish to cut apart the strip, *Bing and Sandy,* into separate words. Also write the word *up* with a capital *U* on the reverse side as you did with *The.* Explain that the word has a capital when it is part of a title. Make a little card with a period on it to use when needed. Follow-up: Give your child p. 27 from the *Reading Work Pages.* In the top section, direct him to draw a line between each pair of words that is the same in each box. . . .

SCIENCE: *Modern Science*, p. 26. Read the questions printed here, and let the child answer them by pointing to the correct animals and naming them. Then continue with these questions:

1) Which have claws? whiskers? antennas? scales?
2) Which animal has neither feet nor legs?
3) Which animals would feel warm to the touch?
4) What do you think each one eats?
5) Where do you think each one probably lives? (in a tree, near a pond, etc.)

GAMES AND ACTIVITIES: Help your pupil to make a basket in which he can keep word-slips.

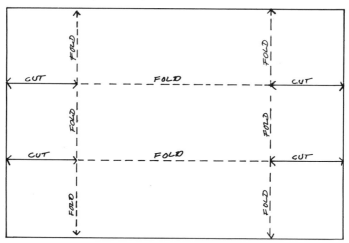

Have him cut on solid lines and fold on dashes. The three sections of each end can be pasted, stapled, or sewn together. Attach the handle. The basket should look like this:

SIXTH GRADE *LESSON 2*

READING: *Lorna Doone* was written in 1869 by Richard Doddridge Blackmore; the present version is an adaptation. Glance over the book, look at the pictures, and try to guess in what period of history the story takes place.

Read chapter I and then answer the following questions: 1) In what month of what year and in what place does the story begin? 2) How old was John Ridd at the time? 3) Why did the boys think his cousin, Tom Faggus, was a hero? 4) Who was John Fry? 5) What do you suppose was the untruth John Fry was telling?

To the Home Teacher: The note at the back of *Lorna Doone* does not indicate that we consider your pupil a retarded reader. The book is included in the Course because it is a good story which children of your pupil's age enjoy. It is hoped that the reading of this adaptation will make him eager to read the original some day.

GEOGRAPHY: Familiarize yourself with the worktext, *Life in Lands Overseas,* by reading the "Contents" on p. 2. Notice that the book is divided into eight units. Each of these units teaches new geographic ideas; the first three deal with physical geography, while the last five deal with the regional geography of Europe, Asia, the Pacific lands, and Africa. . . .

How important are maps to you? Do you ever use them outside of school studies? Where besides in your school books have you seen maps? What were they used for?

The map is the sign language of geography. Begin to review the language of maps by reading pp. 3 and 4 of the worktext. Be sure to learn the spelling and definitions of the terms printed in bold type.

Now work exercises D, G, and B, on pp. 9–11, in that order.

Notes to the Home Teacher: The work exercises given with the lessons should be checked both for geographic accuracy and correctness in English usage. Words misspelled should be corrected as well as geographic errors. The student should do as much of the correction as possible. . . .

LESSON 3

ARITHMETIC: Begin a review of fractional numbers (the idea) and fractions (the name for the idea) by reading p. 12 and doing the "Oral" exercises.

It is convenient to have names for various kinds of fractions in order to indicate whether the fraction is larger or smaller than 1. Review these names on p. 13 and answer the exercises.

Fold a piece of paper exactly in half. Into how many sections of equal size is the paper divided? (2) What may you call each section? $\left(\frac{1}{2}\right)$ Color one of the two sections and fold the paper again to form four sections of equal size. Into how many sections of equal size is the paper now divided? (4) **What may each part be called?** $\left(\frac{1}{4}\right)$ How many fourths are colored? (2 fourths) Is the same amount colored as before? (Yes) Therefore $\frac{1}{2}$ and $\frac{2}{4}$ name the same amount. These are equivalent fractions.

Read p. 14 and complete the exercises. Extend your understanding of equivalent fractions to include the use of computation in forming other equivalent fractions. Complete p. 15.

HISTORY: The first part of each history period should be devoted to a review of the preceding lesson. Here are some questions which your Teacher might ask you about lesson 1: How have scientists discovered how prehistoric people lived? What three gifts did early man have that the animals did not have? What two things did the earliest people spend their time doing? What is meant by the Old Stone Age? the New Stone Age?

Study today pp. 8–15.

SPELLING: Today learn these special words: *history, prehistoric, scientist, mammoth, weapon, upheaval, metal, bronze, furnace.* Then study col. 52 of the *New Calvert Speller* and have your Teacher dictate the words to you. If you have little trouble with spelling, your Teacher may "hear" you spell the words orally but she should not do this unless you are naturally an excellent speller.

Ask the Teacher to dictate these sentences; write them carefully: He handles the car well, putting on the brake carefully and never dashing ahead carelessly when he passes another car. On its arrival at the wharf the crew of the ship stayed aboard.

Your Home Teacher should review the sentences which she has dictated to you, and you should correct any errors.

ART HISTORY: This year you will read about the history of sculpture from the earliest times to the present. The statues and other forms of sculpture pictured in the text are famous, so famous that you can find people who are familiar with them in every civilized country, and they should become well known to you. . . .

If you would like to see how it feels to be a sculptor, you might try carving a cake of soap. Clay also is a material good for sculpturing. In fact sculptors used many different materials: clay, marble, stone, ivory, gold, bronze, and wood. Clay was the first material used. Can you think why?

Begin your study today by reading chapter 1 of *A Child's History of Art—Sculpture.* Find Egypt on a map and try to remember what you may have read in your history and geography lessons about this old country. Learn these terms: sunken relief, low or bas relief, high relief or half round, and full round. Be sure you understand what these terms mean. Try to remember at least three characteristics of Egyptian sculpture.

COMPOSITION: The subject today is "The Fire Makers," based on today's history lesson.

Never start to write a composition until you have decided what you are going to say. Plan the story, and plan the paragraphs. A composition in the Sixth Grade Course usually divides into three parts or paragraphs: (1) introduction (2) main story or body (3) conclusion. Sometimes, however, two paragraphs, and occasionally three, are needed for the body. Here is an outline suitable for "The Fire Makers":

    1) Introduction: How man first learned to use fire

    2) Early ways of making fire (This may be divided into two or even three paragraphs.)

    3) Conclusion: Results of the knowledge of the use of fire.

With this outline in mind, decide what you are going to tell in each paragraph. When you are fully prepared, close your book and write the story.

LESSON 4

ARITHMETIC: Complete these statements:

1. A fraction having a value greater than one is called an _____.
2. A fraction having a value less than one is called a _____.
3. A numeral composed of a numeral for a whole number and a fraction is called a _____.
4. The part of the fraction which indicates the number of equal parts into which a given quantity is divided is the _____.
5. The part of the fraction which indicates how many of the equal parts of the given quantity are being considered is the _____
_____.

If you missed any of these or needed help, go back and re-study pp. 12–15.

Study the illustration at the top of p. 16; then read the page to learn how to reduce a fraction to its lowest terms. When you work the "Written" section, be sure your work follows the sample shown in the second column. Show each step. The first one is worked for you:

$$\frac{4}{8} \div 1 = \frac{4}{8} \div \frac{4}{4} = \frac{4 \div 4}{8 \div 4} = \frac{1}{2}$$

Fractions may be changed to higher terms and to lower terms:

$$\frac{1}{2} = 1 \times \frac{1}{2} = \frac{2}{2} \times \frac{1}{2} = \frac{2 \times 1}{2 \times 2} = \frac{2}{4} \text{ (Higher terms)}$$

$$\frac{2}{4} = \frac{2}{4} \div 1 = \frac{2}{4} \div \frac{2}{2} = \frac{2 \div 2}{4 \div 2} = \frac{1}{2} \text{ (Lower terms)}$$

Replace n with the numeral that makes each of the following equations true. Use multiplication or division depending upon whether you are changing to higher or lower terms.

1. $\dfrac{5}{6} = \dfrac{n}{12}$ 4. $\dfrac{18}{6} = \dfrac{n}{2}$ 7. $\dfrac{27}{36} = \dfrac{n}{4}$

2. $\dfrac{8}{16} = \dfrac{n}{32}$ 5. $\dfrac{25}{35} = \dfrac{5}{n}$ 8. $\dfrac{4}{5} = \dfrac{24}{n}$

3. $\dfrac{7}{2} = \dfrac{28}{n}$ 6. $\dfrac{18}{9} = \dfrac{n}{12}$ 9. $\dfrac{18}{36} = \dfrac{1}{n}$

Answers: 1. $\dfrac{5}{6} \times \dfrac{2}{2} = \dfrac{5 \times 2}{6 \times 2} = \dfrac{10}{12}$, n = 10, 2. n = 16, 3. n = 8, 4. $\dfrac{18}{3} \div \dfrac{9}{3} = \dfrac{18 \div 3}{3} = \dfrac{6 \div 3}{2} = \dfrac{6}{2}$, n = 6, 5. n = 7, 6. n = 36, 7. n = 3, 8. n = 30, 9. n = 2

SPELLING: Study col. 53 of the *Speller* and these special words: subject, predicate, grammar, sentence, eclipse, galaxy, numeration. Do not let your Teacher dictate these words to you until you are sure you have mastered them.

To the Teacher: Sit beside your pupil as he writes his spelling words and the instant he begins to miswrite a word, stop him and do not permit him to provide himself with an erroneous model of the word. After the spelling lesson is over, teach him any words that he did not know.

GRAMMAR: In your own words tell your Teacher a definition of a *sentence.*

Every sentence has two parts, the subject and the predicate. Learn to spell these two words.

What part of the sentence is the subject? What part of the sentence is the predicate? Study sections 3, 4, and 5 of p. 2 in your text, and learn these definitions:

    1. The subject is the person, place, or thing talked about.

    2. The predicate tells something about the subject.

Work orally exercise 3 on p. 2. Complete the following exercise by drawing a vertical line between the subject and predicate in each of the following sentences:

    1. Stars shine.
    2. Our team finally won a game.
    3. The lion was very thirsty.
    4. Every water hole was very dry.
    5. The speed of the boat is thirty miles an hour.
    6. Her hobby is stamp collecting.
    7. The king of the beasts gave a mighty roar.
    8. Many brave men went to war.
    9. A dark cloud casts a shadow.
    10. A field of tall corn grew on the farm.

the pupil working two to five hours a day, five days a week), but the pupil can progress as rapidly or slowly as seems best.

A word about tuition fees: It's $80 for kindergarten; $140 each for grades one through seven; $150 for grade eight. Calvert strongly advises you pay an additional $70 a grade for a teacher's advisory service, which means that a Calvert teacher will guide and comment on the child's progress. (Without this service, Calvert cannot supply transcripts of grades to other schools or testify that a course has been completed to their satisfaction.) You can make special arrangements with Calvert to ship the materials by air when you're cruising overseas—you pay the extra shipping costs.

This is just a bare-bones look at Calvert. For more information you'll want to write them at Tuscany Road, Baltimore, Maryland 21210. If you're cruising with children of high-school age, you may want to contact the High School Extension Division of the University of Nebraska in Omaha.

You may also want to read *The Voyage of Aquarius,* a painfully honest account of a not-so-ordinary family's joys and problems in an Atlantic crossing. It's written by Matt and Jeannine Herron, together with their two adolescent children, so you get the viewpoints of both generations at each point. The daughter's unhappiness early in the voyage—she clearly would have preferred to be in a nonpitching house on land, her parents realized—was hard to deal with, but its resolution and the obvious growth of these four people is a very practical lesson for would-be world cruisers. There are some good notes on classwork on board and fighting the bores. Jeannine, for instance, encouraged both children to keep biology notebooks—sea slugs alone kept the kids entranced for several days with observations of their eating habits, egg laying, and even copulation. (The publisher is Saturday Review Press/E. P. Dutton & Co., 1974.)

Cruising with Children:
A Mother's Viewpoint

Eight years ago, when they were in their early thirties, John and Susan spent a year and a half cruising with their four children, ages ten, seven, and two (the two-year-olds were twins). The boat was a 61-foot ketch-rigged motor sailer built in 1932 by Hodgdon Brothers in Maine. Outside of fitting hammocks above the children's bunks for toys and adding awnings for tropical cruising, the family found they had to make few modifications to the boat. Cruising with four very young children did present some problems, Susan told me:

"Actually, the boat made our decision to go to sea. We had dreamed. Dreams are fun and good to talk about, but everyone dreams. Then one day we were in Florida for a convention and went to Fort Lauderdale to talk to brokers. We asked for a boat that children could live aboard with us, and we were laughed at by all but one broker. So we bought the best and biggest boat we could find. John quit his job to go—he later returned to it when we finished cruising.

"We felt we needed the room—ten feet to a person—because there were six people. A large boat like ours really needed a professional crew at times. Often, John and I would both be on deck tending the boat, and then there would be no one to look after the kids. Once we abandoned a thrash to windward from Grand Turk to San Juan because we didn't feel we had the manpower and we were both tiring.

"Togetherness was a problem. I had four children, two in diapers. I couldn't send them out to play. I couldn't tell them to play at the neighbors' because there were no neighbors. No way I could get a moment of peace except if I climbed the mast.

"I don't think I'd do it again with such young children. The twins don't remember much now. The two older girls remember being barefoot a lot. Never having to wear shoes was great! The oldest girl still writes to people she met while cruising, but the second oldest doesn't remember a great deal except watching porpoises.

"Porpoises, by the way, were always a reason for interrupting lessons. The kids loved to watch them. That and another boat or ship passing, or a barge going by on the waterway. I used the Calvert School to teach them, and we'd stay on deck in good weather for classes. We had no problem enrolling the kids in school again after tutoring them with Calvert. The schools on the Florida coast especially are quite familiar with it. When we moved back to Missouri, we did get some "what's that?" because in the Midwest, it's mainly military personnel who use it. But we had no real problems. The books we used from Calvert were way ahead of their time.

"The days went sort of like this: John would get up very early. Woke me at four A.M. with hot coffee and we'd get under way while the children slept. Then I'd go below, wake up the kids, and fix breakfast. They'd play. Oh, we learned knots together. Maybe they'd tow a toy boat astern. We also had a portable battery-powered TV on which we sometimes picked up local stations. This was great on rainy days—worth its weight in gold. After lunch, the twins would nap and the two older girls would have their lessons. These lasted about two and one-half hours. Occasionally, we'd get crayon walls below when the weather was bad, but it wiped right off.

"We did a few things people don't usually recommend. I didn't tie the kids down. A friend who taught sailing at the Coast Guard Academy was the only one who agreed with me. He said not to tie them down because they'll learn to depend on the line and it can break. In the whole time, only one kid fell overboard and that was at dock. I also used swimming vests from a toy store. They weren't CG approved and couldn't keep the kids' heads above water, though they did provide flotation. But I liked them for deck use because they were partly net and very comfortable. Another nice thing is that they were sort of like living in pillows. The kids couldn't hurt themselves bumping into things.

"Boredom was a real problem at times. We did take quite a few toys. Anything that could fit in a hammock was acceptable as long as it was a toy that couldn't rust or chip easily. I also took a large number of paperbacks along. Someday, I'll write a book myself. Toilet training on a boat with three heads when all three break down on the same day!"

Part II.
Finding Shelter

4.

BUYING A BOAT ISN'T LIKE BUYING A HOUSE; IT HAS MORE IN COMMON WITH GETTING MARRIED

In Florida a few years ago, I met a couple from New England living aboard a Hinckley Bermuda 40, a boat that was a blue-water cruiser from bow to stern, except when you looked at her bottom. There was enough weed growing on her to choke a power mower and the couple admitted, a little shamefaced, that she hadn't been out of the slip for a *year*. For all practical purposes, they could have been living on a houseboat, enjoying the same sunsets without the hefty investment in a well-built cruising boat.

This isn't an oddball story. It's surprising how many live-aboards start out with dreams of sailing around the world and end up at a tropical dock, sipping Mount Gay rum—and dreaming. Then there is the other side of the equation: the fellow who sets off on a world voyage with a boat built for cocktail parties and gentle cruises on the Sassafras River. One family crossed the Atlantic, just barely, in a well-known fin-keel production boat that all but fell apart after two Atlantic gales. The wall-to-wall carpeting was about the only thing keeping it together.

The gap between expectation and reality explains why the first boat bought as a liveaboard is sometimes a mistake. Add to

This shippy-looking Colin Archer, built in Sweden, is typical of "character" boats. You can spot them by their bowsprits, canoe sterns, baggywrinkle. They're often slow but sturdy cruising boats, although the trade-off is invariably restricted space belowdecks. This particular boat has little room below.

this the fact that too many people move aboard without a good trial-and-error stint on any kind of boat, so they're unprepared for the tight corners, the dampness, the constant gentle roll of the boat at the dock. Even a couple of weeks on a chartered boat before you buy can be a good lesson on what your priorities are. Sometimes, you have to compromise.

For instance, I met a retired pharmacist in St. Petersburg who cruises up and down the East Coast on a sloop-rigged motor sailer. Crew: two cats. With any encouragement, he'll disappear into his aft cabin and come up with a bunch of brown photographs showing a bronzed, younger edition of himself at the helm of the graceful double-ended ketch he lived on for some years. She was a Herreshoff design, that ketch, and he is quick to tell you what a wonderful sailer she was, "But not so comfortable. She didn't have the headroom this boat has." The new boat's 10-foot beam, aft cabin packed with books, and open helm station make her a comfortable compromise. She's the same length as the old Herreshoff—30 feet—but she seems twice as big to her owner.

Another compromise was decided on by a couple who cruise most of the year in the Bahamas and the Virgins. They first lived aboard an Alden-designed Challenger yawl, then decided to switch to a 39-foot custom trawler designed by George Stadel. "Switching from sail to power was the big decision," says the husband, "but we found that in the same length boat, we actually had much more space with a trawler type. Also, during the time we lived on the yawl in the Bahamas, we found that we made eighty percent of our passages under power. Now that we're on the trawler, we find that's it's more adaptable to hold conveniences we want to install, like better refrigeration."

Oddly enough, I found two people switching boats around the same time at the same Miami marina. Both were bachelors. One was moving *off* a houseboat and onto a Le Comte ketch because he wanted something "more blue water." The other was moving off a Columbia 29 and *onto* a houseboat "for windows and fresh air. Living in a sailboat can be like living in a well."

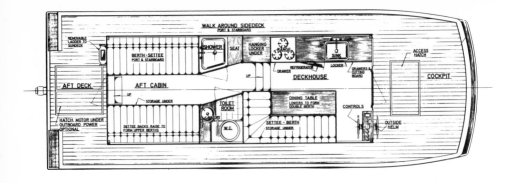

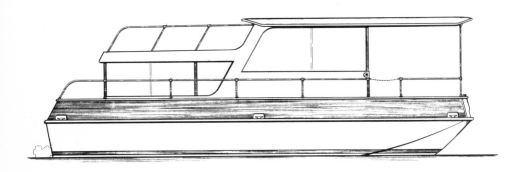

This roomy houseboat is just that—like a house—but if that is your choice, you must sacrifice on sailing ability.

A boat, like a husband or wife, is a very personal choice. There are any number of books on what constitutes good construction in a boat, and how a cruising boat should be equipped. But added to these factors, the potential liveaboard has to make some decisions about how livable the boat is. Here are some of the points to think about:

1. Does the boat have enough stowage space for personal gear? Older boats have the edge here because they were built in an age when cabinetry work was cheaper to install. Today, it's expensive to build stowage into production boats, so the builders stint on it. Don't despair, however, if your new boat has the usual meager hanging locker and bin-type stowage. Just

find an old carpenter who's looking for odd jobs and have him carve some stowage out—or better, do it yourself.

2. Will your sex life go to hell? A big, comfortable double berth and room for same is essential. If you have children, make sure there's adequate privacy. A center cockpit boat—if you're into sail—is often a solution because it provides a good bit of separation between forward and aft cabins.

3. Is the head usable, or merely adequate? If you can't shave comfortably, or if you can't sit on the toilet without scraping your knees on the bulkhead, forget it. You'll be miserable every time nature calls.

4. Is there headroom? If you have to stoop every time you go forward, your posture and disposition are going to suffer. Make certain you can move freely around the boat without feeling cramped, particularly if you're tall.

5. Can the galley handle your ambitions as a cook? There should be lots of good, easy-to-clean working space, nothing dinky or undersize. The sink almost always is a sore point. If you can't fit your pots into it properly, rip it out and put in a good, deep stainless-steel sink. Also, make sure there is a trash bin or room to put one. Most production boat builders assume you toss it in the water, apparently—they rarely include a place to put your trash.

6. Can you read comfortably? Face the fact that you'll probably have to invest in additional lighting, especially over berths and in the galley. New boats and old ones alike—all built primarily for weekend sailors—rarely have adequate lighting.

7. Is the boat easy to maintain? Surfaces and materials should be practical. Unless you don't mind the elbow grease needed to maintain it, don't get involved with a boat that's largely painted and varnished wood inside.

Remember that boats, especially modern ones, are built as toys, as pastime activities, not as homes. Some compound the problem by being badly built, from their inadequate hull/deck joins to the rough finish of their bilges. Then there are the ideal boats—for their owners. These liveaboards explain why their boat is the best choice for them:

Small Family / "Home-Built" Ketch

Joe and Norlene Niemier worked on their 56-foot ferro-cement ketch *Cobia* at a hull yard near Costa Mesa, California. There, you find a lot of organization dropouts finishing bare hulls or, like the Niemiers, building their boat from scratch. When I met Joe and Norlene, they were a few months away from launching. But they had already been living on *Cobia* for nearly a year because they were losing too much time commuting from home to the boatyard and wanted to keep on working through the evenings. With them came their 14-year-old daughter, Libby, a high-school freshman.

On the outside, *Cobia* is shippy-looking, but belowdecks she's a garden room—all white trellis, pale green and white upholstery, and lots of space. The Niemiers decided early in the game that they would be happier living on a boat that reflected their own taste. "We didn't like the interiors of any of the new or old boats we looked at. The layouts seemed poor and the interiors drab. Would you, in your right mind, decorate your home by lining the walls, floor, and ceiling with teak or mahogany? Then cover every seat and couch with fuzzy, itchy tweed? I don't think so. Especially if you only had an occasional window, hardly big enough to put your arm through.

"The solution was to build our own boat. My husband and I did it ourselves in three and a half years working full time. That includes making the mold, building the hull, shaping the mast, making the stainless-steel hardware, and just about everything else. I may be the only woman listed as Master Carpenter on the Documentation papers.

"A great advantage to building your own is that by the time you're finished, you know every part of the boat. We made sure the engine, generator, and wiring are fully accessible, something you don't find on a lot of stock boats."

Small Family / Starting with a Bare Hull

Norman and Susan Elarth and their son Edward, age 13, fell in love with the water during five years' cruising in their Trojan 28, a twin-screw powerboat. But that wasn't the boat they wanted to live on full time.

"We wanted a boat for long-range cruising," says Norman, "so we decided on a sailboat. We also wanted one large enough to overcome the feeling of confinement that most designs seem to have by trying to crowd everything into a small area. Headroom for a six-foot-four man was a trying point—that wasn't even on the boards of designers when we started looking eight years ago.

"As a custom-built boat was out of our range, we decided to buy a hull and finish the interior to our own specs. The kit boats of today were unheard of at that time, but we finally heard of the Del Rey Fifty, a fiber-glass bare hull designed by Bill Crealock. Just what we had been looking for, except we had decided

Another option is a big motor yacht, like this Seaton design, which will never be at the mercy of the wind, but dependent on the fuel tank instead.

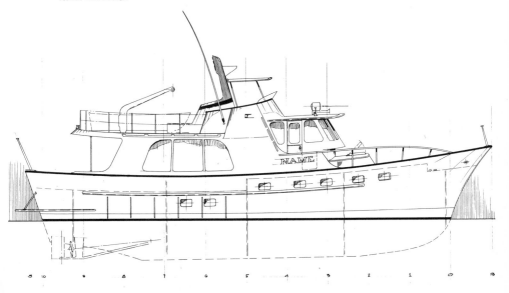

on forty feet as the limit we could handle financially. After a good deal of soul-searching, we decided that if we moved aboard as soon as possible, we could make it. We made a deposit to lay up the hull at the date of my retirement from the Los Angeles County Fire Department.

"We decided on a fiber-glass monohull after examining a number of possibilities. Cement hulls, at the time, were having electrolysis problems and it was difficult to seal the hull. Wooden boats could get worms. Multihulls, such as catamarans and trimarans, could turn over in bad weather. Fiber glass gives you minimum maintenance. That and simplicity of operation and self-containment were what we wanted. We also wanted a boat we could handle ourselves, which decided us on a ketch rig with a club-footed jib."

Says Elarth reflectively: "Speed in itself was never a consideration. Only to be able to go where we want with confidence."

Couple / Double-Ended World Cruiser

"We wanted a sailing vessel we could live on, not a home we could take sailing sometimes," says Bob Bicknell. For him and his wife, Betty, home for two winters in Rochester, New York, was a Bristol 30. Then they went searching for the largest interior they could find in a full-keel double-ender, that could be sailed by either of them alone (Betty is five feet, 105 pounds), in any weather, under all conditions. It also had to be capable of going around the world, which is their aim. They finally settled on Thomas Gillmer's design, Southern Cross, as built by Ryder in Rhode Island.

Because the Bicknells live aboard in the cold north during the winters, they paid special attention to fitting out a boat for cold-weather life. They had completely carpeted the inside of their Bristol with Ozite, a nylon carpeting with a high density foam back, glued to the hull with contact cement. With the Southern Cross, this hasn't been necessary: "*Home,* as we

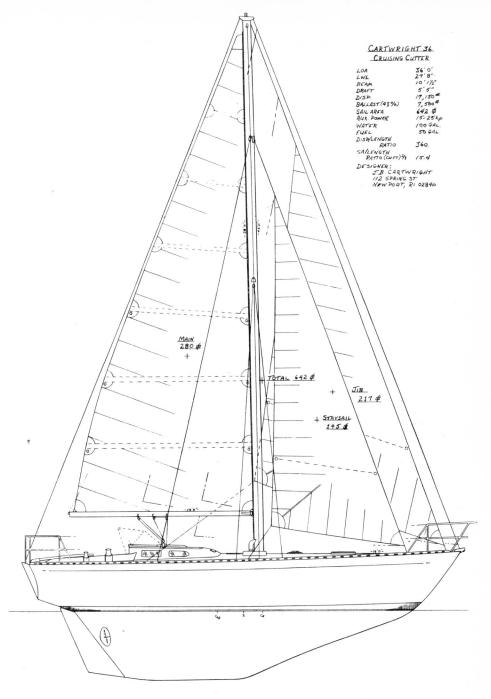

CARTWRIGHT 36
CRUISING CUTTER

LOA	36' 0"
LWL	27' 8"
BEAM	10' 1½"
DRAFT	5' 5"
DISP.	17,150#
BALLAST (43%)	7,500#
SAIL AREA	642 ◻
AUX. POWER	15-25 hp
WATER	100 GAL
FUEL	50 GAL
DISP/LENGTH RATIO	360
SA/LENGTH RATIO (CU FT)⅔	15.4

DESIGNER:
J.B. CARTWRIGHT
112 SPRING ST
NEWPORT, RI 02840

MAIN
280 ◻

TOTAL 642 ◻

JIB
217 ◻

STAYSAIL
145 ◻

This handsome Jerry Cartwright-designed cutter might be your choice if you want a boat to sail around the world in.

named her, is heated with two electric heaters, totaling 1,700 watts, even though the interior is some thirty-percent larger than the Bristol. There's no extra insulation and no condensation whatever, due to the Airex core of the hull. We've been warm and comfortable and walked around in our bare feet at minus fourteen degrees."

Two Friends / 37-Foot Trimaran

Ted, a 49-year-old architect, and a friend have lived on his Vagabond Mk II trimaran since 1970. With her generous 20-foot beam and six feet three of headroom, the tri has a lot of living space, but there is some controversy over whether a multihull is a safe offshore boat. Ted has his own answer to that. "I cruised and raced monohulls for twenty years, but after two years' research, I decided to build a tri. It took me three years and I never regretted the decision. All boats are compromises—like people—and not one is perfect. True, tris are controversial, though I did sail mine to Panama and back, from San Francisco. I'll limit myself to their merits for living aboard —*some* of them.

"I'd have to say stability. This means dinner at anchor in forty knots of wind, in four-foot waves. No fiddles or gimbaled stoves. I realized this the night I watched a monohull rolling and pitching at her mooring while I served dinner for six.

"You have inside spaciousness and light. One thing I really appreciate are permanent bunks, not seats made into bunks. On my boat, six people can have their own personal bunks and storage, so I don't have 'camping' when I have guests.

"Deck space. There's room for twenty people, for folding sails, for two dinghies. And storage—almost too much.

"The thirty-inch draft is a real advantage when I'm cruising. It gives me more options than a monohull has when anchoring and gunkholing. Finally, the weight is about a fifth that of a comparable monohull. My boat's easily driven by a light en-

A stock production boat, the Southern Cross built by Ryder in Rhode Island, is home for a Rochester, New York, couple. The day this photo of *Home* was taken, the temperature was 4 degrees outside, but 70 degrees inside.

gine, so I have less fuel consumption. I can use lighter ground tackle, cleats, lines—all this means less money and fewer headaches.

"A problem is that it's not easy to find a berth because of my tri's beam. If you can get one, it's usually an end berth. This doesn't bother me because I really prefer to anchor out. Some people would consider this a real drawback, because you have to do without phones and power hookups. It can be inconvenient—but it is cheaper."

Retired Couple / Vintage Cruiser

When Roland and Janice Smith retired a few years ago from the staff at the University of Connecticut (he was teaching; she was a librarian), they decided to try living aboard, but to do it in stages. They spend about half the year aboard *First Edition*, their present boat, and half on shore. Roland believes strongly that "plunging" into liveaboard life is fatal, because of the disappointments that can crop up when you try to match yourself to a boat.

As a case in point, the Smiths' first boat was a 34-foot auxiliary, but one winter's cruising down the Intracoastal and around Florida convinced them that she was too small and slow. Their solution was a 40-foot Huckins built in 1950, which they feel has only a few drawbacks. Of course, they couldn't bring the family piano with them, but Roland took up the clarinet: "It's smaller, just as satisfying. I don't know what the neighbors think, though. I don't want to ask!"

Roland says: "We chose the Ortega Forty because it has a reputation for being well designed—no pounding or blue water over the bow—and well constructed. It's of double diagonal mahogany planking, and Huckins controls temperature and humidity during the building process to prevent warpage.

"It's also well laid-out for living. We like the large cockpit, the ten- by twelve-foot 'living room,' and the fact that two can cook or wash dishes at the same time in the galley. Some good, small touches are the vitreous china washbowl in the head, large overhead hatches in the galley, fitted screens on all the openings, and bunk cushions with innerspring construction."

As Roland points out, the Huckins is old, but she gives them the satisfaction of knowing she's one of the best available. Nice feeling.

Couple / Older Fiber-Glass Cruising Sailboat

Unlike many liveaboards, Katie and Gene Hamilton didn't plan to stay aboard forever. They bought *Gusto*, a Rhodes-designed Pearson 41, with the aim of taking a year off from teaching careers while they were young (both are in their early thirties) and seeing something of America. After 5,000 miles of coastal cruising and island-hopping, they found the only important adjustment they had to make was having their life determined by the weather. They also learned to deal with crises: Gene saved a drowning woman; a boat nearly sank one night at the slip next to them; they were almost run down by a freighter.

Gusto never disappointed them, however: "We wanted an older fiber-glass boat as opposed to a new one, which we feel can be outrageously overpriced, underbuilt, and lacking in any warmth or character. After examining several boats, we decided

One thing any liveaboard boat needs is good natural ventilation provided by Dorades set high on the deck, vents, and opening ports like this solid bronze one. Even a big powerboat outfitted with air conditioning needs openings for those times when the system is not operating.

that *Gusto* combined the amenities we wanted (like refrigeration) with a well-built hull capable of long-distance cruising."

Couple / Full-Keel Cruising Ketch

When Douglas Montgomery retired as dean of a medical school, he and his wife, Jane, wanted to go cruising and they thought long and hard about the boat they wanted. *Blue Eagle III*, their Dickerson 41, was the result. Douglas outlines the criteria they set out:

"We wanted a worldwide capability in a boat that could be handled by two people. This meant we also looked for maximum livability but accommodation for only two, though we can sleep two more in the forward V-berths if we ever need crew. This proved a problem, because all stock boats have too damn many berths and no real option to change the interior.

"We also wanted a fiber-glass hull for safety and maintenance, an all-teak interior, and the ability to specify rigging and interior details."

Jane takes up the story here, "We couldn't find a used boat to suit our needs. We didn't want an ex-racing boat, and we did want an aft-cabin, center cockpit boat. Of the stock boats we looked at, the ones in our price range were either badly built or couldn't be customized, so it narrowed down to the Gulfstar 41, Allied Mistress, and Dickerson 41. We opted for the Dickerson because it was built nearby (Trappe, Maryland) and we were able to set her up as we wanted." That includes stowage space for their British hand/electric sewing machine—Douglas built a sewing table for it with a varnished seat.

Couple / Trawler-type

Ralph and Martha Fiske spent about half a year looking for the right boat after they decided to move on board. They settled on a 32-foot Grand Banks designed by Robert Newton and built in 1965. When I talked to them in Marina del Rey, California, they summed up their choice this way:

The Fiskes, a retired California couple, live on this trawler-type named *Marty*, which was used in filming, and also appeared in, the movie *The Young Nurses*.

"This one is wood and has a single Ford diesel, so there's no explosion risk. It has all the facilities of a house and everything is on one level with the sleeping quarters separate. We looked at Owens and larger gasoline-powered boats, which cost less, but we didn't want a step-down galley and a gas engine."

This is just a sampling of the types of boats people live on happily. I've also met a couple who cruised for two years on a 27-footer, a Connecticut man living on a vintage 1920 70-foot cruiser, a family of five on a Westsail 42. The list goes on and on.

We mentioned the Smiths who live on a Huckins. When they retired, they got a bit bored, so they decided to put out a little newsletter called *Homaflote*. It costs $3 a year to get four news-letters (address is Homaflote, Box 336, Wickford, Rhode Island 02852), and I mention it here because it's written by liveaboards for liveaboards. It's an ongoing discussion of which boats work, and what you can do to make them work a little better, as floating homes. If you're contemplating living aboard, it's a good $3 investment.

One thing you learn from people already into this way of life is that the initial investment can be high. How can you afford the type of boat you want? That's a recurring dilemma.

A Worksheet for Liveaboards
on Where to Look, What to Look for

Problem One: Illustrating the $$ Escalation Theory

This is the money you want to spend: $_____

After looking for a month or two, this is the price range of the boats you like and that appear to be floating by their own efforts and not sitting on the bottom:

$_____ to $_____

Typically, what you can afford is nowhere near what you want to spend. So, how do you save?

Solutions

1. Deal with the owner. Brokers pull a ten-percent commission on boats under about $50,000, and that has two consequences for the buyer. First, the owner hopes you'll absorb some of that ten percent by paying more for his boat than he would have sold it for privately. The owner who might sell privately for $8,000 or $9,000 thinks in terms of $10,000 to cover the commission. Second, the broker will do what he can to jack up the price to increase what he makes.

Where do you find boats for sale privately? Maybe the best source is *Soundings*, the monthly regional newspaper whose editorial section is largely a means of filling in the space between its classifieds. You can pick it up at marine stores, newsstands in boating areas, and marinas occasionally, or you can get a subscription to one of the five regional editions. The addresses:

Box 210, Sudbury, Massachusetts 01776
Second Street at Back Creek, Annapolis, Maryland 21403
Box 210, Island Heights, New Jersey 08732
Box 22484, Fort Lauderdale, Florida 33335
Box 510, St. Petersburg, Florida 33731

Call fast on any boat ads in *Soundings* because the best bargains go to the first callers—it's like looking for an apartment in New York. And don't be distressed if it's November 15 and you can't find the November issue on a newsstand; *Soundings* follows a fitful publication schedule understood only by its mailroom.

The Woodenboat, a bimonthly out of Maine, has pretty extensive coverage on maintaining and restoring wooden boats, and it's probably worth the hefty $1.75 cover price to get John Gardner's thoughts on tools or superb color photographs of a Caribbean cruise in a wood Tahiti ketch. If you take wood seriously—and the converts are True Believers—forget the newsstand and get a subscription for about nine bucks. Along with the articles you get a small classified section that's occasionally a gold mine. Address is Box 268, Brooksville, Maine 04617.

Another special-interest magazine that occasionally has a real gem of an old cruiser advertised is a little thing called *Antique Boating*. This is a chatty, ingrown magazine unless you're interested in Kermath engines and Fay & Bowen launches, but a warning—it's easy to get hooked on gracious ladies and you can occasionally live on them. The address is Box 199, Cleverdale, New York 12820.

National Fisherman is really a trade publication for the fishing industry, but you'd never know it. They run some of the best articles on design, maritime history, and boatbuilding, and some of the most irascible articles around on the environment. The classified section lists mainly commercial boats with the occasional pleasure boat thrown in. You can find an honestly built, round-bilged and deep draft workboat suitable for con-

Examples of ads you might find in any of the major boating publications.

version, if your interest lies in that direction. It's interesting that the so-called trawler yachts popping up at boat shows these days are just adaptations of workboats that previously were available privately only by custom building or conversion.

There are also some regularly published boating magazines available at newsstands.

Finally, when you're looking for a boat for private sale—ask. Some boat owners have their vessels sitting around for years, use them occasionally, and have at the back of their mind the idea of selling, only they haven't done anything about it. A friend of mine noticed a 45-foot wood ketch sitting in a Staten Island boatyard in late May after most other boats had been launched. He jotted down the boat's registration number, got the owner's address from the State Registry, and wrote him about buying the ketch. It turned out that the owner was a retired seaman in his seventies who hadn't used the boat for a couple of seasons and, yes, he supposed it was for sale.

To get an idea of current prices of used boats and dicker with a passel of owners at one place, you might want to spend a day at a used-boat show. Yankee Boat Peddlers (259 Water Street, Warren, Rhode Island 02885) started one of these in Newport, Rhode Island, a few years ago, then added another in Galesville, Maryland. They're held in May and June, and they look like a regular boat show with the difference being that the boats are used and put up for display by their owners at fees ranging from $5 to $7 a foot. The larger boats are generally in the water.

You always haggle, of course—the owner expects it, even enjoys it provided you don't irritate him by setting the price impossibly low. Start too low and you're insulting him and his boat and he's just as likely to order you off the dock, something no broker would ever do. I knew one owner who scotched a sale of a $35,000 boat because the buyer quibbled over his choice of a popular radio direction finder—it hurt the owner's pride. How low you want to set your offer depends on the size of the boat, what condition it's in, where it is, and the time of year. I once surveyed about a hundred people who had sold boats recently and found that 31- to 36-foot powerboats sold for $1,000 to $5,500 less than original asking price, while 30- to 35-foot sailboats went for $1,000 to $4,500 less than the asking price.

If a boat was put up for sale in the spring and still hasn't sold by the fall, desperation sets in and the owner may as much as halve his price rather than face winter storage charges, deterioration of the boat over another season, and maintenance drudgery again in the spring putting her in selling shape again.

If you're young, handy with tools, and don't mind the continuing maintenance, wood boats are still the best bargains, provided you can get a good survey on one. Dry rot isn't always a fatal problem, incidentally. A friend of mine from Colorado bought a good 28-foot wood sloop for $2,500 simply because her transom was rotted, possibly from heat buildup from the engine combined with water accumulation. He took her down to Maryland's Eastern Shore, had a builder there replace the transom for $350, and spent a year in the Caribbean on the boat with no further rot problems. Rot can lower the price of a good boat dramatically, but unless it is extensive and has infected the basic structural members, it can often be remedied.

2. Buy a boat that's been lived on before in your climate. Let someone else with money fix the problems.

3. Buy in the right place at the right time. The best bargain time in the Northeast and Pacific Northwest is in late fall. A boat that was put up for sale in the spring and looked at by a dozen tire-kickers unwilling to meet the owner's price may still be for sale in the fall. By October, when he's putting down the $50 deposit on winter storage, he's really getting nervous.

I talked to a man who owned a 46-foot Huckins, built of wood in 1952, priced at $23,000 and unsold after 12 months. Why? "Difficulty in inspecting her. Our town is the last frontier of the Texas coast and too far for most people to travel. Also, folks don't want to spend money on boats in this custom/ elderly/luxury class."

Certainly wooden boats like this Huckins are harder to move

in the South where the hot sun and marine borers present maintenance problems, so they may sell below what they would in the North. Another point is that backwater areas can sometimes spring bargains in big boats. Buyers generally resist traveling over 50 miles to inspect a boat, so a large vessel parked in a small-boat heartland isn't going to draw the same response it might in a big-boat heartland. Just recently, I heard of a 35-foot houseboat and a Luhrs 33 selling far below their book value because they were located in the boondocks—one in a small Georgia town, and the other in upstate New York with its short boating and buying season.

4. Pay cash or pay as you go. It's not necessarily cheaper to build a boat yourself or refinish an old or damaged boat, but it has a built-in checks and balances system. It's almost impossible to finance a building project unless you have other assets (in which case, you probably aren't worried about cutting corners anyway), so if you build yourself, you pay as you go. A slogging method, but after a few years, the bank doesn't hold an expensive mortgage on your pride and joy.

Just how expensive boat financing can be is demonstrated by these figures. The first two boats were home built, the second two were paid off in cash from savings, the last two were financed. Since banks consider boats toys, you can't get a long-term, house-type mortgage on a boat. You get a five-, seven-, or ten-year mortgage with heavy interest charges.

Cost Per Month	Original Price of Boat	Family Income	Remarks
$3	$4,000	$2,000	The most extreme example. Here is a young man living on the hook near San Francisco on a boat he built himself, paying cash for the materials as he went. The $3? Kerosine for his stove and lantern. He points out that apartments in his area typically rent for $250 a month and over.

Cost Per Month	Original Price of Boat	Family Income	Remarks
$41.25	NA	$11,000	Economy living in Honolulu on another home-built boat, a 27-foot cutter. The young couple pay $30.25 a month for their slip and an additional $5.50 a month each as a liveaboard fee.
$100	$18,000	$10,000	This 41-foot trimaran in St. Petersburg is paid off, so the young family on board have only a monthly slip rent of $88 plus $7 to $12 a month for electricity.
$132	$16,500	$25,000	The boat, again in St. Petersburg, is a new 43-foot production houseboat for which this couple in their forties paid cash. Their monthly cost breaks down into $120 for a covered slip, about $12 for electricity.
$555	$35,000	$25,000	The monthly charge reflects the high cost of a boat loan on a cruiser bought at 25-percent down with a seven-year payoff period. Covered dockage in St. Petersburg runs this liveaboard family $98 a month with $27 a month for electricity. The monthly payment on the loan is a substantial $430 a month.
$792.75	$75,000	$28,000	The boat, a 55-foot motor sailer, was an expensive one and the monthly payment on the boat loan runs $735 for the couple who live aboard with one child. The loan aside, their actual monthly expenses run about $41.25 for slip rent, plus $5.50 a month per person.

Not quite a project that started from scratch, *Wind Borne* was built from a bare hull by her owners Gary and Terri Foulger.

5. Build it yourself—partly. The next chapter is all about finishing a bare hull, a popular expedient today. Just a few words from Teri and Gary Foulger, who are living on the Cascade 42, which they finished. "We knew what kind of boat we wanted," says Teri, "but our pocketbook couldn't afford something like a Cheoy Lee, and the affordable production boats were poorly built." So they decided to buy a Cascade hull because they were familiar with the builder.

"We both saved every penny we could, sold *Onrust* [their 29-footer] and bought the new hull. Gary worked four days a week as an electronics engineer to bring in money. The other three days and many evenings, he worked on the boat. I worked on the boat full time, fiber-glassing, painting, varnishing, sanding, and buying materials. After two and a half years, we were finished.

"Despite all the hard work and frustration, it was well worth it. We have the boat we want."

5.

BUILD IT AT HOME—PARTLY

Nothing is more basic or satisfying than building a boat, as Noah found out when he pegged his treenails home. Building a boat from scratch, whether in steel, wood, fiber glass, or a new construction material like C-Flex, is the subject of whole books, which discuss it much more fully than we can here. But we can talk about shaving costs by building a boat from a bare hull, that is, buying a hull and finishing the deck and interior yourself.

Although the "kit boat," as it's sometimes called, has really blossomed in the last ten years, it's not a new idea. It's simply a logical solution for people who can't afford a finished boat, yet don't have the time or confidence to translate a table of offsets into full-size lines, or who want a fiber-glass boat without the investment of making a mold or plug. During the Depression, a lot of people bought unfinished schooners built in Nova Scotia and brought into America with unfinished interiors —cheap housing, and it still is.

You can do the same today. Out in Costa Mesa, California, you follow the highway away from the sea, turn off at a deserted factory, and bump along a road to a ten-foot-high slat-and-chicken-wire fence. Roll back the fence at the point where it overlaps itself and you're face to face (bow to bow?) with two great Westsail 32 hulls, looking trim and orderly in the clutter of lumber and tools around them. Climb up on one of these hulls, stand on the just-finished plywood deck, and you see that this chicken-wire enclave is surrounded by heaps of 200-pound truck tires, all being noisily moved around by a creaking forklift. What are the hulls doing here?

Well, they're here because of the tires. Bob Gates and his friend Al, who own the hulls, bartered off their time as watchmen at the tireyard in return for a place to work on their boats. Like the Depression liveaboards who finished their own boats from bare hulls, Bob and Al are following an economic imperative—this is the only way they can get the kind of fiberglass cruising sailboats they want. Depression liveaboards were keenly interested in shelter, but Bob and Al add some other imperatives. These boats are vehicles to the kind of adventure they want to find in the South Seas, Alaska, or wherever the whim takes them.

The dream demands a lot of sacrifice. The two of them shave a lot off their personal expenses by living in shacks built in the lee of their boats—a strange juxtaposition, something like an eccentric millionaire keeping his Bentley stored in a lean-to. I had a cup of coffee with Bob in his shanty. Inside there's some secondhand furniture that can be discarded without too many qualms when Bob, his wife, and child move on board permanently, and, here and there, the flash of something shiny and new. Invariably this is something meant for the boat when she's ready to launch, like the handsome brass-cased barometer. The shanty, Bob explains, is really a kind of test tank. Here, he and his wife try out some of the equipment they've bought for the boat and decide whether or not it will work. They've already been through three different types of stoves in their kitchen. They figure if it doesn't work in the land kitchen, it'll be worse at sea.

Bob and Al have refined bartering and scrounging to a fine art. It's difficult to run your hand over anything on either boat without one of them piping up, "They cut that piece the wrong way over at Westsail, so I picked it out of the discard pile. Fits pretty good. I just added a little piece here."

Bob Gates inside his Westsail 32 bare hull. This is about what he started with.

One thing Bob and other bare-hull builders learn is that the $6,000 they may plunk down for a hull doesn't buy instant Tahiti, but what looks to be a giant bathtub with a bow and a transom. Yes, they do save money, though at a proportionate investment of time and sweat. And they won't end up with a 45-foot ocean cruiser for $15,000. The hull is just the start, and it will be months of work and thousands of dollars before the interior takes shape, the sails are in the locker, and you hear the reassuring slap of the halyards against the aluminum mast.

The time and money you save depends on how large a boat you want and what kind of kit you are working from. The phrase "kit boats" is unfortunate, conjuring up memories of those airplane models you built as a kid. The original "kit," as marketed by Luger, Clark Craft, and others, has everything you need to finish the boat, often packed neatly in a crate (although Luger now sells one-piece hulls instead of hulls in pieces that have to be assembled). These companies specialize in kits for family sailing, but most of the companies we have listed in the appendix mainly sell completed boats; selling bare hulls is only a sideline.

Types of Kits

Frame Kits

One step above building a boat from scratch. You buy the frames and other critically measured parts, so you don't have to do any lofting. Clark Craft sells this type of kit.

Boat Parts Kit

All the parts for the hull, interior, and deck, all premeasured, precut, and ready to go. You follow the detailed instructions and plans and put everything together—young kids have built such boats without great problems. Luger has a few fiber-glass parts kits for sailboats large enough to live on.

Bare Hull

You buy the hull, then finish the boat over a period of months or years, depending on the size of the boat. A number of builders solicit this kind of business, and some production yards will pop a hull for you if their schedule permits.

Bare Hull and Then Some

Few people buy just a bare hull. In fact, unless you're an experienced builder, it's probably a bad idea to start with anything less than the hull with deck, ballast, engine, rudder, and bulkheads. Just about any builder who sells bare hulls will custom finish it for you to any stage of completion, with the proviso that the more they do, the more you pay. A few companies have standardized production of partially finished boats, offering what they call Sailaway Kits, Liveaboard Kits, or Power-Away Kits. The Sailaway, for instance, as offered by Westsail and a few others, gives you everything except the engine and finished interior. The boat is operational, but Spartan.

Some Backyard Advice

If you're serious about buying one of their hulls, most builders can put you in touch with owners who have finished the same boats. Obviously, they're not going to steer you to anyone who's grumbled about the hull, but you can count on getting fairly straight answers to your questions. Be cautious, though, in talking to owners who are also dealers for the boat they're living on. The boat may be just what you want, but try to get the opinion of someone who's not biased.

Even if you're interested in a cruising ketch, don't hesitate to talk to a guy finishing a power cruiser from a bare hull. You'll run into many common problems: finding raw materials, locating a place to build, buying tools. James Henry of Seattle had built three boats from scratch when he, his wife, and his tools

Bob Gates and a friend work on his hull in a padlocked enclave surrounded by a tireyard in Costa Mesa, California.

moved aboard the hull of a Spencer 53 ("It's like carving out a homestead!"), but he still found it useful to swap ideas and sources with other builders: "They know who has what and have already traveled the road you're following."

I talked to a number of people around the country who have finished hulls, and here is what they advise beginners:

1. *Build a bookcase, then build a pram.* If you can't build a bookcase, you can't build a pram, and you certainly can't finish a yacht. We're not saying you have to be an expert to start—though most builders have previously built boats or have had extensive shop experience—but you do need dexterity and the ability to use your head. As one builder put it: "It's easier to teach an intelligent ignoramus how to use glue and nails than to fight the bad habits and prejudices of a skilled man."

If you can, spend time in a boatyard, something infinitely more instructive than reading books. In fact, one boatbuilder has his bare-hull buyers spend a day at the yard glassing up their bulkheads so they go away with a feel for fiber glass.

The big problem in starting without a lot of experience is that you have to spend so much time thinking about what you're going to do next. Then you worry whether you're doing it right. Mauri Pelto of Juneau, Alaska, a rank amateur ("Well, I've built kitchen cabinets and bookcases") who finished an Ingrid 38 from Blue Water Boats, says he had no problem learning on the job. But he adds: "In retrospect, I think it would have been cost efficient to have a pro do one area, such as the library table and seat, and the joinery and glassing around them—*to set a standard.*"

2. *Buy as much of the boat as you can.* There are several good reasons why you should let the factory handle jobs like casting and installing lead ballast, bonding the deck to the hull, installing stringers, putting in the engine pan and engine, and so forth. These not only demand special equipment or skill, but they're critically important for the structural integrity of your hull. For instance, a plastic hull is quite a flexible animal and it can be bent out of shape by careless handling, so you should certainly let professionals install the floor and some of the bulkheads.

Another point: How much frustration and time can you afford? That hull you're buying is an enormous shortcut already. You could spend eight months building a 40-foot hull by yourself, but the men at the yard turn one out in about a week. By the same token, those workmen can cut all your interior patterns in a couple of days and sell them to you as a kind of subassembly kit. If you want to spend this additional money, you can spare yourself a lot of delay. The whole project comes down to a giant balance sheet, with your debits (money) against credits (savings in time). Remember that slow progress can be very demoralizing. Having the ballast, tanks, bulkheads, and engine installed by the builder costs little in terms of money, but they are a big hassle if you try to do them yourself.

3. *Use professional help when you need it.* Placement of the engine, the sail plan, the installation of fuel and water tanks—all these affect the sailing characteristics and stability of your boat. If you want to depart from the plans, invest a few bucks in a naval architect and follow his advice. It may save you from that curse of the amateur boatbuilder—wanting to incorporate every new plan you see.

4. *Choose a place to build carefully.* First priority is always closeness, because if you can only work weekends and evenings, you don't want to burn up an hour or so just getting to the hull. If you can plunk it in the backyard, fine, but check out your neighbors and local zoning laws.

Before Mike Mullins had his Westsail hull shipped to his St. Louis, Missouri, neighborhood, he went over local ordinances and learned he needed a permit that would allow him to

A St. Louis neighborhood where Mike Mullins's hull arrives and draws a few spectators. Later it roused some complaints from neighbors who didn't want the big hull sitting in a local backyard.

keep a recreational vehicle in his backyard. The town called a hearing, notified the neighbors whose yards bordered on Mullins's place and, since there were no complaints, duly gave him a permit. His hull arrived and was carefully squeezed into his 50-foot-wide yard and angled to stay the statutory ten feet from the property lines. The nextdoor neighbors still had no complaints, but people living a few houses away went to the town council and created a mild uproar. The tale ended happily thanks to many of Mullins's neighbors who signed a petition saying they didn't mind having the hull around, and thanks to some sympathetic people at city hall; but be aware that these problems can crop up.

A nearby marina or boatyard (providing the owner doesn't insist on having all work done by his own men) can be an excellent place to work, supplying you with a travel lift, 110V power, water, compressed air, and even sympathetic advice. Some yards on the West Coast where bare hulls are very popular specialize in hull storage, and you can find a dozen or so hull owners working on different production boats in one place. Sometimes, the builder of your hull can supply space, either free or at a charge. For example, when I talked to Medford Starrett at his yard in Florida, no less than eight owners were working on hulls; he leases fenced space for his 45-footers at $39 a month.

Industrial lots, warehouse compounds, local businesses—canvass all of these. Small firms may have unused space in their lots and be willing to lease you some of it, provided you're neat, tidy, and trustworthy. Just knock on doors until you find a businessman willing to listen.

Wherever you settle, make sure you can get water and electricity year-round. And, naturally, if you're working in the northern latitudes, you'll want a work space that's under cover and can be heated.

5. *Gather your tools.* The bare minimum is a collection of good quality hand tools: hammers, screwdrivers, pliers, T square, and level. Next, you'll want at least a band saw, table saw,

power drill, jointer, and orbital sander. Invest in carbon blades for the table saw and carbon steel router blades for the drill.

Power tool kits made by Gilliom Manufacturing (1109 North Second Street, St. Charles, Missouri 63301) are good, and they are not expensive. Gilliom supplies plans and important parts for band saws, table saws, belt sanders, and more.

Remember that books are tools, too. Appendix A lists a number that you will want to read.

6. Know that you're going to get discouraged. When I asked one backyard builder if he was ever intimidated by the project, he told me, "No, but I sure as hell got frustrated." Remember, too, that no matter what people may promise in the way of muscle power, raw materials, and skills, they probably won't keep up their enthusiasm for the job. The only thing that stands between the empty shell and a finished boat is you.

7. It's going to be tough on your family. "You see a lot of divorces among boatbuilders," a middle-aged engineer told me. He and his wife have been working for four years, side by side, on their boat and she's nearly ready to launch; but they know the road hasn't been easy for some other couples in the Costa Mesa area in California. Of all the amateur projects started in this building heartland (and here we include boats built from scratch), maybe one in five or six is finished. And along the line, a lot of marriages or friendships break up. Often enough, the men and women working on a hull don't understand how long it will take or how much money will be eaten up by that fiberglass "bathtub." ("I started to hate it after a few months," one woman who split told me. "One day, I dropped a plank on my toe and I got so mad, I started kicking the boat keel. They thought I was going nuts. Maybe I was.")

A fellow on the East Coast, still happily married, told me frankly, "The one derogatory thing is taking a lot of time away from your family. I spent a thousand hours working on my hull over a year and a half [he finished a 36-footer]. Think about it. A thousand hours is a lot of time to be away. I missed things my kid did when he was growing up, and I missed a lot of time

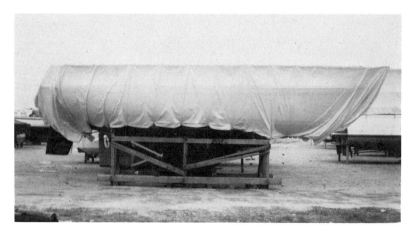

An economical way to protect a partially completed hull over the winter is to use a cover like this made of synthetic cloth; the cost is about $85 from Stamford Packaging (Box 3081, Stamford, Connecticut 06905).

with my wife. Even when you go home, you pull out catalogs looking for this part or that part. Or you say you don't feel like going to a party because you want to work on the boat or because you're tired. It's a strain."

8. *A bare hull usually costs more to complete than you antici-pate. Be pessimistic!* A man made his living by driving a de-livery truck for a Kansas grocer, so he had to watch every penny. When he bought a Westsail 32 hull, he found out that it would cost about $1,300 to have it delivered from California to his Midwest home. No deal, he decided. He borrowed a pickup truck and a flatbed trailer, drove to California with a friend, and the two of them carried the hull back to Kansas. They couldn't do over 40 miles per hour, but the man didn't care. Instead of $1,300, he paid out just $400 for wideload trailer permits, gas, and a lot of hamburgers at truck stops.

How much you save by finishing a hull depends on this kind of ingenuity, a talent for scrounging, and, most important, an ability to get deals. The markup on marine hardware, electronic equipment, compasses, and all the rest is considerable, so many hull buyers either use their builder's discount (most hull builders will extend their discount to you and order the equipment for you; a few add a service charge to cover their trouble) or incorporate themselves as builders. As you are legitimately finishing a boat, you can set up a company (after all, you may want to do this professionally), print some business cards, and get about a 40-percent discount on most of the things you'll need. Even better, set yourself up with some other builders so you aren't pestering manufacturers with a bunch of small orders.

What will you actually spend? That depends on your experience and the level of finish. I talked to four people finishing Ingrid 38s, William Atkin's cruising design as built by Blue Water Boats at a finished cost of up to $60,000. Remember, we're figuring the builders' time at zero, not $10, an hour:

a. A 52-year-old man who had little woodworking experience started with the hull, deck, seven bulkheads, and engine installed. He worked only on weekends and usually three evenings a week, with no outside help (except for machining the pintles and gudgeons for attaching the rudder).
   Time: 3,000 hours over a two-year period
   Cost: about $30,000

b. This Ingrid was completed by a man with 20 years' experience in boatbuilding, both private and commercial. He started wtih the hull, ballast in place, and engine installed.
   Time: 600 hours, working full time
   Cost: about $22,000 to $24,000

c. This hull was finished by a 35-year-old journeyman boatbuilder and his 28-year-old wife. He started with the hull only, and worked on the boat from four to seven each day and on weekend mornings. He advises taking a month off each summer to do something else.
   Time: 4,500 hours over a three-year period
   Cost: about $18,000

d. The last hull was finished by a man who had worked on a couple of dinghies and a 17-foot trimarian. He got some

help from two friends with no prior experience, and he
started with the hull only.

Time: 6,000 hours over two and a half years

Cost: about $24,000

9. *Realize there are some special problems in financing a bare
hull*. Most backyard builders report problems in getting a bank
to finance an unfinished boat when there is no collateral like a
house or land to back up the loan. In some cases, parents or
other relatives have guaranteed the loans, or the hullbuilder
has financed, though this is a rarity. If you can, the best way
is to pay cash as you go, for the hull, tools, and materials.

A Mississippi banker who finished a bare hull himself told
me, "Our bank policy would be no loan on a kit boat not yet
completed. However, if the customer can qualify for a loan on
an open basis, or if he has other collateral, the loan can be made.
We have financed boats that were completed by someone else
and being bought by bank customers."

Where to Find Bare Hulls and Kit Boats

It's possible to make arrangements with many builders, especially small yards, to pop a hull from a mold that would otherwise be idle. Some companies *specifically* solicit bare-hull business or are specialists in the kit boat field. In almost all cases,
they've had experience with builders, and though they can't
hold your hand through the entire operation, they do know
what the problems are and can give you a reasonable amount
of advice. Regional boating publications may mention local
builders who also want this type of business. And, if you're
interested in finishing a boat in England, look up the July,
August, and September 1975 issues of *Boat* and the December
1975 issue of *Yachting World*. These have guides to a number
of British companies offering everything from Cornish crabbers
to steel canal craft.

A list of boatbuilders who supply kits and/or bare hulls is
provided in Appendix B at the back of this book.

6.

THE FINE ART OF MAKING
A SMALL BOAT BIG

It starts with subtraction—off-loading the stuff you don't need. Next comes the process of fitting in what you do need. The fact is a boat has a lot more space than the average weekend sailor realizes, but the space has to be turned into storage. As you'll see, if you're looking at newer boats, it's cheap to build space into a boat, but expensive to build in storage—think of the hourly wages skilled carpenters are getting in yards these days. The best solution is to find an old carpenter who works cheap or designate yourself ship's carpenter and think up some ways to add storage compartments.

You won't have a giant problem with an old boat (low wages in the good old days means the older cruisers have tons of carefully constructed storage spaces). This is what one lucky woman says about her aging, but lovely Atkins-designed motor sailer:

"This boat sold itself on storage—tons of it. I do miss a little more hanging locker space, but not enough to weed out old clothes. We have a desk in our stateroom and a chair that hangs on a hook when not in use. Also, there are shoebags nailed to the bulkheads for slippers, boots, shoes. The drawers in the galley have a second row after the final stop—this utilizes the curve of the topsides."

Filling Up Wasted Air

One liveaboard sewed three-inch-deep pockets in her cabin curtains to eke out stowage space for small hard-to-find items like sunglasses and pencils. Another, "homesteading the ocean" with his wife and six children, decided he had to have a bathtub. He built one into the main cabin's table on his 48-foot trimaran. Others have set up a photographic darkroom in the forward cabin, a lapidary shop in a rope locker, a woodworking shop in an unused cabin or head.

I've seen clothes rods in shower compartments and kitty litter boxes in the bilges. One of the most ingenious uses of space was in the forward cabin of a 36-foot ketch. The liveaboard family had clothes hung from the overheads, stopping about 15 inches short of the berths. Any guests could wriggle into bed just under the dangling hems.

Conceivably, you could fill every nook and cranny of your boat, but aesthetics are important when you live aboard. As a veteran sailor told me, "You can get very depressed after living for a week in a storage bin."

More important than appearances is safety. For instance, on a sailboat you don't need standing headroom in every corner, so it's convenient to lash unwieldy objects like a rolled awning, fishing pole (encased in a PVC tube), even toilet paper, and paper towels overhead. Mounting heavy objects overhead, however, can in extreme cases change the balance of the vessel and lead to problems in bad weather, when something can fly loose and become a dangerous missile in the cabin. On one boat, a fellow had his folding table stowed above, where it was securely held by four latches. A problem occurred when a friend was visiting and put the table back up one day without fastening all the holds. The table was jolted down that night and nearly killed the skipper.

Maybe the best way to start planning stowage is to think about the different ways there are to keep things in place.

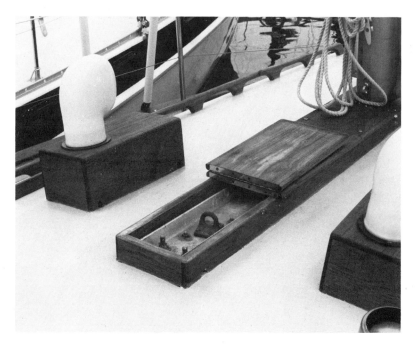

One way of adding some stowage space on deck. This small locker could hold winch handles and spare blocks, for example.

Remember that stowage is a two-way street: The item has to be safe and also at hand. I asked a man who's single-handed his 30-foot cutter around Maine and the Caribbean for about eight years about stowage, and he gave me a quick tour of his boat as an example:

"I cruise, mostly offshore, throughout the year, so everything is slanted toward seagoing capability rather than creature comforts. I want to know that I can reach for something in the dark and it will be in its place.

"People who come aboard usually comment on things like this—my binocular rack within easy reach of the chart table. Or the sextant stowage behind the chart table so the sextant is instantly available for that opportunistic sight when the sun is playing hide and seek with the clouds.

"There are things like my cracker stowage tins, kept right next to the stove. That keeps them dry and crisp. And I have the handle for the second bilge pump stowed right above the chart table, so when the occasional sea comes aboard in messy weather, it's a matter of seconds to draw the handle from the rack, insert it in the socket, and pump her dry, all from the companionway.

"There's nothing ingenious about the way my boat is laid out. It all results from experience. She's been owned by people who cruised and they put a modicum of thought into her and hit upon the right solutions to different problems."

Solutions to problems—maybe that's what stowage is all about. Stop and think for a moment: How many ways are there to stow items so that you take advantage of wasted space? Maybe you can think of two, three, four ways after a moment's thought. But that's just the beginning.

Drawers probably come to mind. Ironically, these are one of the great wasters of space on any boat. A weekender may find them handy, but for a liveaboard, they're space extravagant,

A sail locker that makes use of empty space under the cushions of the forward cabin in the Aurora 40, a Canadian boat.

giving you around 30-percent *less* usable space than a bin in the same area. Opt for bins wherever possible and, if you can specify it, make them top- and front-loading so you can get at items stowed at the bottom more easily. For instance, build in a couple of doors on the front of bins under your bunks—they can go quite deep.

If you prefer drawers, make them as big as possible (one possible exception being the flatware drawer where you do want to keep the cutlery from sliding around). A number of small drawers eat up about 5-to-10 percent more space than a couple of big ones.

When the Marois family took me through their cruiser *Butch* in Florida, they were particularly pleased with the custom-built drawers under the forward V-berths. Because of the V configuration, the very deep drawers could only be pulled out about half their depth, and it took a little reaching to get at the back of them, but the owners figured the inconvenience was worth the gain in space.

Hanging lockers are nearly always inadequate for liveaboards unless they've been custom built with year-round living in mind. Opt for as wide and deep a locker as possible. The depth is important because you don't want your clothing chafing at the shoulders every time they swing with the boat's movement. A wide locker has the built-in advantage of giving you larger door areas to work with, and there's a lot of space that can be used on the backs of doors. For instance, you can put shock-cord straps on the doors to hold rolled-up clothing or bed sheets. You can also use the space for those same plastic pouch-type shoebags you used at home. If you don't have doors, bulkhead spaces can be used the same way.

Net hammocks are invaluable stowage in the galley and over the bunks. They're light, use space over counters and berths that's generally wasted, and they're self-ventilating. A small (36-inch overall) cotton fishnet hammock swinging from the overhead and filled with fresh apples, bananas, and oranges gives you some relief after a few days of living out of cans. Keeps the crew regular, too.

Slide-away stowage is another alternative that lets you take advantage of wasted space; in this case, narrow spaces with some depth behind them. This is especially handy stowage in the galley where you need more working room a few times a day. When Dick Zaal designed the compact Contest 25, for instance, he took advantage of a deep space right above the companionway step to fit in a sliding breadboard. You can make a similar arrangement below a countertop, and you might want to add a chain to the end of the board that can be fastened overhead to a hook to give you an added measure of support.

If you have a vertical space with some depth, you might want to fit a tall narrow drawer, with openings at the side for cutlery or spices, and a small cutting board at the top. Another option is fitting in a kind of tray. About two feet by one foot and a couple of inches deep is a good size. You might want to face the tray with wood that will take a bright finish. An indentation on the side acts as a fingerhold, and a fastener of some type keeps tray in place.

Pull-down stowage, for want of a better word, can be useful if you have equipment you want to keep accessible but out of the way. An example is the photo lab layout I heard about on a 32-foot cruising sloop. The boat wasn't roomy enough to entirely dispense with the two berths in the forward cabin, which were sometimes needed for guests. So the photographer/owner mounted his enlarger on a strong pin over one of the forward bunks. It was tightly secured at the "loose-footed" end and could be swung down when he needed it, and up when he needed the bunk. As long as you use a strong pin and a stout locking arrangement at the foot of the enlarger, this is a reasonable solution.

Doubling the Possibilities

"If you have one thing that does two jobs, that's good design on a boat," says a naval architect I know. With that, he describes a feature of his own 43-foot 5-inch yawl. The entire

Dowel-type stowage on the Colvin-designed *Great Expectations*. You can change the setup by moving the dowels around in the pegboard holes to fit the dishes being stowed. Incidentally, this compartment closes by lifting the door, which then slides up and latches in place. A nice idea.

galley area of the yawl is covered top and front by matched-grain, varnished teak, a lovely piece of workmanship by her Danish builders. It means more counter space in the galley and it also gives a navigator's table to both port and starboard.

The Heritage alcohol stove and oven (manufactured by Paul Luke in Maine) is recessed from the countertop and inboard so that two teak panels cover it top and front. The top panel jackknifes on a piano hinge and can be stowed under the bridge deck. The vertical partition lifts up by means of two slotted handholds (they and three holes at the bottom also serve as ventilators) and stows at the foot of a bunk. This is on the port side.

To starboard, the icebox lid has a projecting ledge inboard and lifts up to allow access to the chest. When the lid is swung up, a bolt slides forward to hold it in place while a crewman loads ice or whatever. This arrangement places all the galley "tools" under wood and gives ample space for preparing food or spreading charts.

Another example of how to make one thing do two jobs, actually three jobs in this case: The idea of a swiveling seat that can be locked in place in three locations was thought of by Dick Austin, who commissioned the design of the Giles 38 (by Laurent Giles and Partners) on which it was used.

Basically, the seat pivots on a vertical stainless-steel tube that is set into the corner of the settee, actually part of a support pillar-cum-grabrail that continues upward in teak to the deckhead. The seat can swing through a 180-degree arc and is locked in position by a handwheel and screw that grips the pillar (a pin set in holes on the pillar can also be used). Depending on its location, the seat works as a cook's seat, a navigator's stool, or as an extra seat at the table.

LEFT: This cutting board on a Contest 25 takes advantage of some dead space over the companionway steps. RIGHT: A tray that can be stowed in a narrow space, in this case over a galley locker.

Doubling up can also solve the old problem of what to do with the boarding ladder. Rather than allow it to take up precious room in your lockers, why not do it European fashion and make the stern boarding ladder part of the stern pulpit (safety rail)? It's done on a number of production boats in Europe and it's a job that can be handled by any competent pipe welder.

On the 32-foot Westsail *Valiant,* John and Betty McConkey installed cupboard doors that are hinged at the bottom. With "stopper" chains, they can be used as convenient countertop work areas when it's time to cook—often clams and fish, which the couple catch off Balboa Island in California.

The McConkeys, like most liveaboards, agree that space is not a real problem on most boats, provided you've bought one with your life-style and interests in mind. As another liveaboard put it, "I probably have more storage now than I did when I lived in a house—mainly because I unloaded all the junk."

Cheating a Bit on the Work

One of the great things about modifying a boat today is that you can be an all-thumbs amateur using only simple tools and still produce some beautiful finished woodwork. The secret is that a few companies are making reasonably priced teak and mahogany accessories for boats; they take care of the tricky and time-consuming assembly jobs and you just screw the stuff in place. Most of these companies produce the old standbys like teak cockpit grates, handrails, and utensil holders, but they also have some clever thoughts on saving space that are worth repeating here. If you're interested in shortcuts, contact these firms for their catalogs.

H & L Marine Woodwork (2965 East Harcourt Street, Compton, California 90221) has been at this business for a long time. They have about the widest range of accessories, including some handy things like utensil divider inserts, library racks, glass racks, navigators' racks, folding ship's ladders, and drawer units. A couple of things of special interest are the undertable drawer and a thing they call the "combination lift shelf and magazine rack." The first is a multipurpose drawer that uses up some of that wasted air under your table. The second is a foldaway shelf that can be swung up to hold a radio direction finder when needed, then flopped down to be turned into a magazine or book rack. There's a seventy-five-cent charge for their catalog.

Marine Artisans (Box O, Chester, Connecticut 06412) is a

Swiveling seat on a Giles 38 works in three positions.

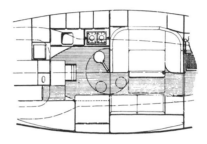

Typical of the kind of ready-made carpentry work available is this binocular box made by Chips & Shavings.

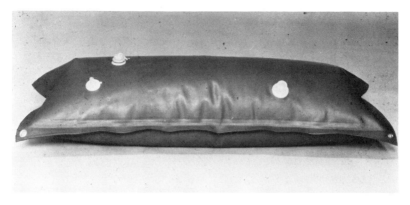

One way of utilizing awkward spaces is a flexible water tank like this one. Installation is very simple because the tank can be folded and can adapt itself to the space in which it is fitted, whether in the keel, bow, or under the seats. Photograph courtesy of W. H. Den Ouden, Inc.

very small outfit that makes some solidly constructed racks. The selection is small, but they will also do custom work—a stowage rack for your hand-bearing compass, perhaps?

K & S Marine Wood Craftsmen (20 Seventh Avenue, Long Branch, New Jersey 07740) work only in teak. They have a number of items, including a handsome book rack that the cruising sailor will like.

Most of the teak accessories made by Seaforce Products (124 Belvedere Street, San Rafael, California 94901) come in kit form, ready for assembly with the brass screws and teak plugs included.

Finally, there's Chips & Shavings (9410 N.W. 13th Street, Miami, Florida 33126), a small company that specializes in teak woodwork, though they also work in mahogany. Send fifty cents for their catalog.

Help from the
Housewares Department

They're not made of teak, but other stowage shortcuts we should mention are plastic containers with tightly fitting lids and Zip-Loc bags. Use these to "segregate" stowage in your voluminous bins. You can buy different sizes and use them for spare screws, engine parts, toilet items, soaps, cereals, and numerous other things. One cruising couple liked the idea of "containerization" so much that they fitted their forward cabin with four 32-gallon-size plastic trash bins with lids. They used two of them for stowing their clothes—dampness was kept out— and the other two for ship's gear. It's instant carpentry on a grand scale.

7.

A GALLEY IS NOT
A KITCHEN

Think of a boat as a limited life-support system. It gives you in an area smaller than the average studio apartment a place to sleep, cook, read a book, or do nothing. And it has these capabilities whether you're daysailing or crossing the Atlantic. You can also think of your boat as a simple machine or a complex one. If you want it simple, eliminate as many possibilities of equipment failure as you can. You really can do without mechanical refrigeration and electric stoves. The ultimate solution is to eliminate the galley altogether, which is what some people claim the British do! In a less farfetched vein, I actually know of a couple living aboard a Clipper 26 in Honolulu who tore out their galley and replaced it with cupboards. As they don't do extended cruising, they decided to eat in restaurants and just keep snack-type foods—fruit, nuts, crackers—on the boat.

That's one way to handle a galley, but it's not practical for most people. Some opt for a very complicated galley with enough gadgets—including a flush-mounted blender—to keep a generator going full bore. Others go to the opposite extreme and have a simple two-burner alcohol stove, a sink with a hand pump, and an icebox—the sort of arrangement you found on every boat 30 years ago. Whatever the equipment, there are certain basics to look for in a galley.

Let's say we were going to design a good, functional galley for a cruising sailboat. Here's what we'd want:

A U shape, so you have something to brace yourself against in rough weather, but it would have to be a *good* U, opening aft, not toward the middle of the boat so you are thrown athwartships in a roll.

No wood, except in the fiddles (rims along the edges). That sounds Philistine if you're a traditionalist, but if the object is easy maintenance on a long cruise, plastic surfaces get the nod. Insides of cabinets, of course, should be well-finished, not rough, so you can wipe them down easily.

About those fiddles, they have to be three inches high to do you any good. Some people prefer fiddles just around the edges

An excellent U-shaped galley in the Swan 65 designed by Sparkman & Stephens. Notice the high fiddles on all the counters, which will keep things from sliding around. There's a safety sling for the cook attached to the right of the stove.

of the counters; others like a few interior fiddles to keep things from sliding around on a big workspace. That's a personal choice. Oh, and the fiddles should be open at corners so you can sweep crumbs off the counters easily.

Rounded corners everywhere (this is true throughout the boat). The edges and corners of fiddles, counters, bulkhead dividers should all be rounded so they won't stab your side in a pitching sea.

Strong grabrails overhead and anywhere else you need them. Look for grabrails where you would instinctively reach when you lose your balance.

A *safe, well-gimbaled stove* with plenty of room to swing, about forty degrees. If you think about it, the galley is a kind of weapon, a place of sufficient hazard to make the cook feel like an endangered species, and nowhere is this more evident than around the stove where you may have to handle hot grease and boiling water. There should be clamps to hold pots in place, a raised rim built around the stovetop to catch spilled grease, a strong bar running lengthwise in front and extended a couple of inches from the stove. This is not only a handhold in a pinch but protects you from being tossed onto the hot stove. Finally, there should be a galley belt, strongly fastened, to protect the cook when working under way. This sling should cradle the buttocks comfortably (you may want to make it wider than the usual surcingle supplied on production boats).

Good bin stowage and plenty of it. The galley is not a place for drawers, except possibly for flatware, and these drawers should be lined with cork or some other soundproofing material to cut the clatter when under way. As for dishes, stack them on top of each other, not racked in those vertical divider affairs. There should be no stowage directly in back of the stove unless you like singed armpits. A useful thing in a galley, and I've seen it only on the Gale Force among production boats, is a slotted section for storing knives. This keeps them from chopping your fingers in that jammed cutlery drawer.

A *kerosine stove*, assuming the boat will be used long-range. Kerosine gives off more heat than alcohol and is cheaper and more readily available abroad (the British call it paraffin). An oven, maybe, but a two-burner with a portable oven that can be set up on top is just as good. If you have an oven, it does make good stowage space for pots.

Deep sinks—two of them—as big as possible. Toy-size ones are OK for Shirley Temple, not for a cruising family with pots and dishes to clean. Faucets should be high enough so they don't rake your hands every time you wash dishes, and the water should be operated by a hand pump. Pressure-pumped water, just like home, is fine dockside but wasteful of water at sea. A foot pump may be preferred because it frees your hands for work. Going offshore, you'd want a saltwater pump and—another nice touch we've seen on a DeFever-designed custom trawler—one of those restaurant-type pumps that dispense liquid soap. It's much easier to handle than a slippery bar, and far less messy.

Cold storage. Really offshore, you won't find ice, but for those times when you do have it, you need a well-insulated icebox—really thick walls, not the flimsy variety usually found on production boats. Dockside, mechanical refrigeration is undoubtedly nice (also nice if you have a big powerboat with room for the generators to keep it humming). Any boat with an AC alternator can handle the larger 115V units, and there are excellent units compatible with 12V battery systems (there are combination AC/DC units as well). A 32V system has the advantage of handling the refrigerator/freezer with a recharge every 24 hours. If you do have mechanical refrigeration, pay attention to insulation again, for poor insulation will make it work overtime.

This is a general tour of a good galley, but naturally few people would agree, even with something as seemingly innocuous and well-used as the cook's belt. For instance, one cruiser I know will tell you categorically that a sling holds you captive: "You can't get out of the way in case there's a bad grease spill. I'd prefer a railing or bulkhead as bracing, but unfortunately you can't always lay a boat out the way you want it."

Something often neglected on boats is a good garbage bin. This one on a Gale Force uses no metal hardware—the wood hook on the back catches under the frame to hold the bin in place.

Another fellow differs with the general regard for kerosine. What about propane, he asks: "It's quick and easy to control. People say it's dangerous and the tanks have to be handled with care, but I work on the premise that if you know something is dangerous, you use more care in handling it, so it becomes less dangerous."

I found a surprising range of opinion about galleys among cruising sailors. Here are a few pointers they would agree on:

Make sure there's adequate stowage. Cruisers practice on a daily basis the fine art of holding down almost anything—noiselessly. "Until you've experienced it," writes one man, "you simply can't imagine the sheer hell of a rattling galley. After a while you learn to distinguish the clink of a jelly jar from the tinkle of the almost empty gin bottle." Of course, you can stuff rags into every crevice, but it's easier to line the shelves with felt or plastic matting.

You've also got to have adequately ventilated bins for bulk stowage, a couple of drawers for small items and cutlery, and shelves with fiddles, and sliding doors (sliding doors are more conservative of space than ones that open). "Drawers are wasteful of space," says a man we talked to. "Open shelves tend to empty themselves or impress guests with how much food you have. One or two drawers for utensils, racks for dishes, canned food in bins below bunks, and dry food in lockers up under the decks—that's how I'd arrange it."

Keeping things in place is a recurring problem. "Anything not properly stowed will not stay put," advises a fellow in the Caribbean. "Even my top-loading refrigerator nearly emptied when my boat was rolled beyond ninety degrees." Some solutions are fitted glass and bottle stowage, slot-type knife holders cut into a counter, divided upstanding containers or drawers for flatware. A flexible arrangement for holding dishes in place lets you move wooden dowels around on a pegboard to accommodate various shapes and sizes.

Choose suitable equipment. If you plan to live at dockside with occasional cruising, then you can afford the convenience of a real "kitchen" with electric stove, refrigerator, and gadgets. If you cruise long-distance, on a modest yacht without generators and the wherewithall to keep them fueled, best opt for simplicity for the sake of self-sufficiency.

Think in terms of what will be available in the way of fuel. Kerosine and butane are cheaper and more available than alcohol. On the other hand, a diesel or wood stove makes sense in northern climes, though not in the tropics where the heat given off is suffocating. One fellow living on board in Canada points out that a stove can do double duty as a heater. He has a Dickenson diesel stove and finds it gives him constant heat, plus an oven for cooking—all at a cost of moderate fuel consumption (about 24 hours' operation on a gallon of fuel).

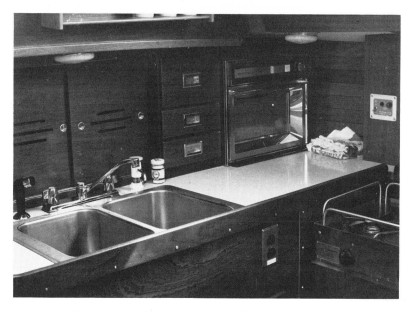

Deep double sink and plenty of workspace in the galley of a Hinckley Southeaster 50.

If you enjoy baking, by all means get an oven. One liveaboard told me she measured the height of her oven before Thanksgiving, bought a six-inch-high, 12-pound turkey, and had all the trimmings for her family of four and four guests.

Remember the basics. Living full time on a boat means the galley has to be supplied as well as the kitchen in a house. Here is a list of what you may want to stock. And as one seasoned cruiser adds—don't forget the cook's gin!

EQUIPMENT LIST

Pressure cooker (4-quart capacity)
Skillets (either cast iron or porcelain-covered cast iron)
Pots and pans (a good quality "nesting" set, stainless steel is best though expensive)
Can openers (take *several,* different sizes and types)
Grater
Rotary egg beater
Spatulas (carry several)

Knives (at least four, different sizes)

Baking pans (at least one each for bread, muffins, cake, pie)

Corkscrews (several—at least one plastic-handled model)

Cooking spoons (several of different sizes)

Mixing bowls (get good quality stainless or porcelain, which can also be used for serving food)

Flatware (service for eight, plus some "junk" pieces)

Tongs

Colander

Coffeepot (also a teakettle, get the widest possible base on both)

Measuring spoons (two sets) and measuring cups

Dinner plates (for eight, and *do* use china if you're cruising. Paper plates are expensive, hard to dispose of, and wasteful)

Mugs (at least a dozen good-size ones for soup and coffee)

Salt and pepper shakers

Glasses (a couple dozen of heavy plastic, plus a dozen of heavy glass)

Spice rack (a wooden one for the bulkhead—as big as possible as you should carry a lot of herbs and spices)

Cooking thermometer

Thermos jug

Vegetable peeler

Ice pick

Part III.
On the Water

8.

FINDING A PLACE TO BERTH— NOT AS IMPOSSIBLE AS YOU MIGHT THINK

A fellow living on a 35-footer in Sausalito wrote recently about the restrictions on permanent liveaboards. Here's what he told me:

"Living aboard is discouraged in the present private harbor, probably rightly so. I wish there was some way genuine itinerant cruisers might live aboard for nine months or so. Anyone more permanently around (this includes me!) can find a place ashore. Otherwise, the harbors fill up with nonnautical types simply looking for quaint, cheap places to live. These should be directed to mobile-home parks. People who don't *use* their boats for the unique things only boats can do should be squeezed out. This might include me, but what the hell. Fair is fair."

This view may be legitimate, but what he's talking about is only one side of the situation. You can find the other on Pier 6 of the Dinner Key Marina in Miami, a pier that looks much like any of the others. The water is free from debris, the walkways uncluttered, and the boats are as shippy as the ones on Pier 5 or 2. Only a few clues, like the bicycles chained to the head of almost every slip and the wooden nameboards on the pilings, give the place a permanent air and suggest that 80 percent of the boats on this pier are liveaboards. When you've spent some

Which of these four boats are being lived on? When I took this picture at Boot Key Marina in Marathon, Florida, there were live-aboards on the trimaran and the houseboat. It's a modest proof that liveaboard boats are pretty indistinguishable from their neighbors—with no laundry swinging from the booms.

time on the pier, though, you notice it's free of those opulent yachts that seldom go to sea and those racing machines preparing for the Southern Ocean Racing Circuit in a suffocating atmosphere of expenditure—the kind of boat mix that seems to dominate in Miami. The atmosphere on this pier is that of a neighborhood.

I was talking with Hope and Martin Miller—he's in medical electronics and she's an artist—on the 54-foot American Marine Admiralty Ketch named *Elysium* that's been home for them and their two young children for four years. While we relax and watch a Florida sunset, a cheerful face with a lot of beard attached appears at the door to the enclosed cockpit. It's Stefan, the young fellow who lives on a small sloop a few slips away. Stefan's the sort of person who munches on carrots and is happy with the money he can pick up doing odd jobs on other boats around the marina. Stefan wants to know if seven-year-old Mark can come out for a few minutes. They've been building a toy wooden sloop and Stefan has just finished rigging it so it's ready to sail. Chatting happily, he and Mark sit on the edge of the finger pier next to *Elysium* and find out how to catch a breeze with a 30-square-inch mainsail in the piece of water the Millers call "our backyard."

The Millers told me that, if they want it, they can "live straight" here. They've had 75 people over for a party and they've had pizzas delivered to Pier 6—just like in suburbia. But the reason they moved on board is the camaraderie of life on a boat—meeting people like Stefan and stopovers from every part of America. It's a different life from on shore. It's getting mail from cruising people you know from Manila and the Mediterranean. It's taking off for a week's sail to the Islands without four hours of driving to the boat and stowing gear. It's the ability to disconnect the electrical lines and leave for a year or three without a house on land to trammel you.

Sure, there are adjustments. "My mother bet my sister I wouldn't last a year," says Hope. " 'How can you leave your garden?' she asked me. The answer is [pointing to the wicker hanging baskets in *Elysium*'s saloon], I brought it with me.

"The hardest part was moving away from a backyard and sidewalks for the children to skate on. Friends were concerned about the kids and frankly so was I, but they're much better off. Their imaginations have blossomed and I can't claim the responsibility. If they can't have enormous toys like the other kids, then they've learned to have as much fun with cardboard boxes and pieces of wood. I've found that children who live on board are more alive, more energetic, more self-sufficient—they've seen and done things other children haven't.

"Our values have changed, for the good I think. It starts when you sell off the bric-a-brac, the silver and crystal that still looks beautiful. My worst moment was the garage sale, but afterward, I felt relieved not to have all that stuff. We did keep a collection of crystal figurines I had as a child, a nice bit of delicacy among our growing seashell collection."

The important question, of course, is would they prefer to live on land again? Hope gives this careful attention and tells me something that happened the week before: "We had dinner with friends and on the way back here in the car, I said, 'I'm really glad we're going home to the boat.' I was remembering all those years of walking through a front door and seeing big, empty rooms."

When I left *Elysium,* it was twilight. Around me boats rolled a bit at their slips as a trawler headed out for an evening cruise, and the only sounds were the slap of waves against hulls and of halyards against masts. Hope and Martin had told me that part of their contentment was in living in a *good* neighborhood, and on this peaceful evening, I thought this kind of life can be addictive if the surroundings are right.

When you move on board, you're not just moving *on* a boat, but *into* an environment. The boat itself can be as perfect as you want, but a run-down, antagonistic environment can sap enthusiasm. Some things to look for in a marina:

• Do the owners care about how the place looks? It doesn't have to be glamorous, but it should be clean.

• Are the owners friendly? Are the people on the docks—weekend sailors or liveaboards—fairly content? Cheerfulness is contagious. If there are other liveaboards, talk to them about the marina management's attitude.

• If you have children: Are schools nearby? Are you in a good school district?

• Is water and electricity available year-round? Would you be required to leave the dock during the winter—as is the case in some northern marinas?

• Can you do all maintenance work on the boat yourself? Some yards require that any repair work has to be done by them and not by yourself or outside workmen who may work for lower wages.

The alternative to living in a marina is to live on the hook in an anchorage, but this is a way of life under attack right now.

Even liveaboards in marinas sometimes don't want to be lumped with their fellows anchored off. I first learned about this "fear by association" on a big cruiser berthed at a marina in the Florida Keys. My hostess and her family had been living aboard this cruiser for about 17 years and she had a genuine rapport with a lot of liveaboards around the country, but the sight of some sailboats moored in the harbor beyond brought her to the boiling point. "Those people who anchor out are freeloaders," she told me. "They row up in their dinghies in the morning to use our water. They're always in our laundromat and the washrooms. They don't pay a cent for anything."

I remembered her words a few years later, talking with a friend who lives on a boat in San Diego with his wife. We got on the subject of San Diego's growing concern with the anchorage area. I knew that holding tanks for sewage were now required on boats anchoring out and that time restrictions on anchoring were being considered. "The welfare boat owners," he muttered. "That's what I call them. We're trying to encourage people to tie up at the docks at five dollars a day or at the yacht clubs. The anchorage was starting to look like a junkyard—you wouldn't believe some of the boats that showed up. They'd drop a hook and stay for months."

Holding tank regulations, 72-hour limits on anchoring—these are a couple of ways shore communities are trying to patrol their waterways. Another wrinkle turned up in Key West when the town passed ordinances forbidding the use of city property for anchoring or bringing a dinghy ashore. If you rowed in for groceries and left your dinghy on the beach, you might return to find it being lifted onto a dump truck! Again, the thrust of the ordinances was to discourage "undesirable" elements from living aboard anchored boats.

Indeed, Florida is a hotbed of regulations these days. Sitting in the cockpit of his big sloop one evening, a Florida liveaboard (in a marina) summed up the situation for me: "The boatman here is forever the villain. He pollutes the water with his little contributions. The towns dump millions of gallons of polluted materials, so does industry, but the boatman is the culprit.

Between forty-eight- and seventy-two-hour limits on anchoring, zoned anchoring, and timed bridge openings, we have a lot of harassment, not only for liveaboards but for all boatmen. Much to my sorrow, I have to admit that some so-called boatmen need these restrictions. So we're all stuck with regulations made by landlubbers who don't know a bow from a stern."

Certainly, opting to live on the hook is a cheap alternative, but it brings with it a certain amount of trauma. A young fellow living on the hook in California passes on this frank advice for people who want to do it: "To avoid trouble, you should look very conservative, don't bother anyone, don't tell people you are living aboard, and be prepared to move on if necessary." He does it because it's possible to live on a small boat anchored out for about a thousand dollars a year, if you eliminate all unnecessary expenses. Right now, he can't afford to live on land.

Although you can get by at anchor for your food costs plus

The free anchorage off Dinner Key Marina in Miami. You might stay here when you know you should be cruising—that's known as "The Curse of Dinner Key."

$3 a week for kerosine, there are some decided disadvantages to living on the hook. Let's qualify that: There are disadvantages if you don't like roughing it.

For one thing, it means doing without electrical hookups (which means you cook with kerosine or another fuel, or you run the generator). It means no dockside water connection; you can always tell the people living on the hook—they're the ones rowing in with gallon water jugs at six in the morning. It means a dinghy jaunt when you have to go to work, make a phone call, buy a loaf of bread, or if you get a craving for butter pecan ice cream.

Advantages? It's quieter at anchor, no clanging of halyards. It's private. It's a shade more secure from thievery. It can be a reasonable alternative for multihulls who can't find a berth or end up getting shoved onto end berths, open to the wake of every passing boat.

Cheaper, maybe, but let's hasten to say here that living outside a marina isn't always free. You can have the security of a permanent address, so to speak, by renting a permanent mooring from a town. A family living on a 32-foot sailboat in the fishing fleet moorings off Newport Beach, California, told me their mooring rent is $192 a year. They also burn up about $3 a month of diesel number 1 for heating, cooking, and lighting, and about $8 a month in gasoline for the generator that charges the batteries so they can have a light and some TV for the kids between seven and eleven P.M. Incidentally, the kids row to school every day!

Compare those prices to the going rates in Newport Beach for berths, which are "what the traffic will bear" or around $4 per foot a month. In addition, berth dwellers in this area (and there are about 13,000 boats in Newport Beach) haven't got binding leases or much assurance of stability in their slips. Worse, boats can be doubled up in slips and suffer similar abuses.

Now, we all know there's a certain amount of *coping* involved in boating today. Like the skiers who live with longer lift lines at Vail and the tennis players who book a court a week in advance, boat owners learn that there's a "Future Shock" to recreation. Facilities can get strained to the breaking point near big urban areas. About the most drastic example is California's Long Beach Marina near Los Angeles where there's a waiting list of 12,000, and you may be on it for ten years before you get a slip.

This all holds true if you own a boat. If you're living aboard a boat, the situation gets trickier. Not long ago, I got a discouraging letter from a family who live aboard in Oceanside, California. They're paying about $250 a month for their berth and they tell me that if they had to make boat payments as well, there is no way they could stay on their boat—it would be cheaper on land. I asked them if they encountered any restrictions on their life and their reply was: "You bet!" "It's time all boating people stood up and were counted," the husband wrote me. "There's a definite trend for the elimination of all liveaboards, and they're starting by eliminating children and pets.

"I happen to think family cruising is the only place left to teach kids responsibility and trust. You mishandle a sheet, a winch, even a dockline, and it could be literally a disaster. The total dependency on your boat and your abilities are an education in themselves.

"We looked long and hard to find a slip before launching, and the restrictions against us and our kids were a thing to behold. We paid ten dollars extra per person and five dollars extra for our poodle a month, in a run-down marina on the L.A. Harbor —and considered ourselves lucky. The last two months, we've harbor-hopped through five harbors looking for a place to stay, and the same old thing. No kids. No pets. No slips. No more than two on a boat. No liveaboards.

"I suppose they want a boat parking lot for income, but keep the *people* out. Most of these harbors are federally funded, yet the lawmakers legislate against people living aboard. The tax base on my boat, though, is the same as on a house and I get the same homeowner's exemptions.

"Newest thing is a move in the state legislature to give preferential treatment to boats that have multiple ownership. That kind of thing really squeezes out the little guy and forces us into public anchorages that are being eliminated as fast as feasible.

"The next step will be us having to move to Mexico or somewhere else out of the country. You can tell I'm getting bitter. Five years' fighting in the Second World War and now they try legislating against my way of life in retirement."

This is a short and rather impassioned insight into the problems of liveaboards at marinas. In the course of writing this book, I visited a number of marinas around the country and I found that about a third of the larger, more modern ones won't take liveaboards at all. The percentage is much higher in popular boating states like California and Florida where there are heavy demands for marina space. You find three refrains among the marina owners:

"They don't support the marina." I was talking with the owner of a big Connecticut marina in a pretty lavish store he runs. As we chatted on a Saturday morning, it was hard not to be aware of the Shetland-sweatered, commuter bunch totting up their purchases for the weekend. Hard to argue with his dollars-and-cents philosophy, which goes this way: "We're set up for the active boatmen. We want them *not* to be sedentary. If they use their boats, it promotes our business in sales, repairs, upgrading of equipment."

I got the same view from the businesslike owner of a big Chesapeake Bay marina. "They never get under way much," he said. "They buy their parts from discount supply houses and do their own work. They don't contribute an amount equal to the trouble they cause." What trouble? "Ah, they're nosy, always looking over your shoulder and second-guessing you."

"Liveaboards are slobs." Unfortunately, some are and it hurts. Time and again, liveaboards told me that no matter how neat they keep themselves and their vessels, they're often lumped with the liveaboards who clutter up the dock, hang their wash out in full sight, and let their boats run down. You're tarred by the same brush.

"They're just trying to get by cheaply." It's hard to stifle the

envy of a fellow on land who's paying $600 a month for an apartment with a view of Honolulu Harbor when you're at a marina a stone's throw away and paying $60 a month. Well, marina owners are sometimes the first to support the land-lubbers. Says an attorney who is a partner in a big California marina complex: "Marinas are not a place of habitation. They're places to moor boats. They involve a substantial capital investment. There's no reason why the boating community should support a few persons who want to live on boats at a cost far less than they would pay somewhere else. We don't believe the Constitution guarantees a person the right to live on a boat for twenty to thirty dollars a month with all taxes and utilities paid when the cheapest living quarters on shore are three or four times that."

Incidentally, in order to brush you off, a marina manager may tell you that there's a city ordinance or a health ordinance against liveaboards. This may not be so. Check with the harbor patrol and the city hall and get an answer, even if it means being switched to a dozen departments before you get one.

If all marina owners thought along the lines of the men we've quoted, liveaboards would be practically outlawed. But there's another side, typified at its best by Bob and Marge Foright who used to manage the Boot Key Marina in Marathon, Florida, before "retiring" on board their old cruiser. Being live-aboards themselves, they realized that there are advantages: Security improves, there are more hands around to help during storms, there's a strong sense of community. They did their best to foster that sense of commitment to a community, even to the extent of throwing "block parties" for the Boot Key live-aboards at the end of a pier. "Any excuse for a party will do," Marge told me during a visit—in fact, I happened to be the excuse that night. The Forights realized that in a real sense the marina becomes a liveaboard's "town," and with any encouragement, he'll try to keep it clean, safe, and quiet. It was a liveaboard at Boot Key who told me, "This shouldn't be the place where you come to raise hell away from your home, because this *is* your home."

One of the strongest arguments in favor of liveaboards—the good ones—is this sense of responsibility. It's generally accepted that the liveaboard areas of marinas have a much lower crime rate than the other areas, so much so that at one San Diego marina liveaboards are carefully distributed so that there are at least four boats on each of the marina's eleven finger docks. This marina also requires liveaboards to have a phone on board for security reasons.

A marina owner in Florida credits liveaboards for helping to track down an arsonist who was setting fire to trees and trailers on his grounds. And another marina owner in Virginia says they've alerted him to boats whose bilge pumps were working too often, to docklines that were frayed or broken, and to boats full of rainwater. They've also helped him during high winds and storms. "You can always use an extra pair of hands in a storm," he says, echoing the sentiments of a lot of marina people.

We could go on with the kudos, but let's just end with the words of a marina owner in North Carolina: "We have about twenty liveaboards at our marina all the time, and it definitely gives the place a nice atmosphere. We have very little theft, and I'm sure it's because of the liveaboards." Incidentally, like the Forights, this fellow is known to throw some good block parties, and about the only rules he insists on are that you BYOB and bring a musical instrument if you play one.

Which brings up the subject of rules and restrictions. Here's what to expect:

A Quota System

Many marinas that accept liveaboards have a quota. At California's Dana Point, for instance, it's 5 percent of the 2,500 slips, which is about typical for a marina that large. At most, the quota is ten percent. There are a few reasons for this, the main one being that marinas don't want to squeeze out the free-spending recreational boatmen, and certainly weekend sailors deserve a slip as much as you do.

Often enough, the managers aren't terribly strict about the quota if you look respectable and really need a place to berth your boat. In some West Coast marinas where slip-renters have been asked to sign a paper saying they wouldn't move aboard, they often found no hassles if they went ahead and did it anyhow. The quotas do tighten up the available slips in popular liveaboard towns like San Diego. There, the manager of one marina keeps to a strict 3 percent quota and says, "Most of our liveaboards have been here an average of five years and have no intention of leaving. We've not been able to accept new ones for several years and I turn down an average of one liveaboard boat a week."

You can circumvent the quotas and additional charges for living aboard by simply moving on and keeping quiet about it. This solution has added a new word to the English language— *hideaboard.* It's an uncomfortable way to live because you're always waiting for the man to tap you on the shoulder. Worst case was a woman in Newport Beach who moved on board, against marina regulations, with her husband and three-month-old baby. Nights were a horrow show of fears that the baby would cry too much and call attention to them.

Pets—With Restrictions

Dogs are banned in a number of marinas, although the ban may be lifted for a cat or some other small, quiet pet (hamsters, turtles, anyone?). Often, a marina will ask that dogs be kept on a leash when off the boat. A California marina owner told me she doesn't mind dogs if they are the "well-behaved, old family retainer type." Small dogs definitely get the nod over big ones.

Children—With Restrictions

Some marinas won't have any liveaboards under 21; at others, the age limit may be 16 or 8. A California liveaboard tells me: "The new Dana Point Marina does not allow liveaboards to have children under eighteen. They are assuming in advance your child is destructive. What big business really wants is 'boat storage.' They don't want you to live in the marina or use it, just *park* your boat there."

Moderation in the Parking Lot

Most marinas have limited parking facilities and they often ask you to follow the "one car per slip" policy. A Florida marina had to have assigned parking, which was strictly enforced, because some liveaboards kept dilapidated, nonrunning cars on the grounds. Enough said.

Keep the Docks Clear

Marinas are fairly adamant about liveaboards not cluttering up the docks with junk. You may be asked to restrict your things to the dock box, or to keep nothing on the dock except a hose and boarding ladder. A Florida marina goes so far as to provide a workbench in a shed so the docks won't get cluttered with handyman projects. Bikes, mopeds, and unicycles should be kept lashed forward on the boat or chained to a designated tree. Ask politely what to do with your stuff and the marina owner is likely to be friendly. Not so if he trips over your bike on the dock one dark night.

Miscellaneous Points

You don't hang laundry from the boom—use the laundromats. And, hopefully, you're not going to pollute your backyard by pumping raw sewage overboard. If you don't want to use the holding tank or macerator-chlorinator, use the marina washrooms. And don't overload trash containers. Finally, keep the noise down after ten P.M.—most marinas require this. Remember that a crowded marina is like a very densely populated, if

expensive, tenement. You and your friends are just a thin wall
and a few feet away from the next boat.

"Difficulties can usually be overcome by providing refer-
ences, being clean, keeping the boat clean. We find the less
we have to do with any marina we are dealing with, the more
they leave us alone. A low-key profile is a help. We don't
party much, nor do we make noise," advise a Seattle couple.

The Added Charges

There are some marinas that charge liveaboards the same as
the weekend sailor, but they're a disappearing minority. Certainly, your electricity will either be metered (with perhaps a
$100 or $200 deposit required) or you'll be asked to pay a flat
additional charge each month for electricity. That's the very
least. Marinas have any number of methods for adding on
charges, with California pioneering a kind of "head tax." Here
are six ways of billing, based on a 35-foot boat. The first three
examples were given me by Florida marinas, the other three by
marinas in California. Charges given are *monthly*.

any 35-foot boat	*35-foot liveaboard boat*
$60	$60 + $22.50 electricity
$52.50	$52.50 + $5 garbage, water, and park- ing
$61.25 ($1.75/foot)	$70 ($2/foot)
$87.50	$87.50 + $25 a month for one person and $15 for each additional person
$35	$75 + $5 electricity
$85.50	$85.50 + $6 per person

In short, extra liveaboard charges can take the form of a flat
charge or some kind of head charge, and they can add 25 percent and up (way up!) to the bill. Obviously, a family living
on a boat at some California marinas will be paying 100 percent

and more a month above the charges for a fellow who owns the weekender at the next slip.

Any discussion of marina charges brings up that pressing question: What does it really cost to live aboard? It isn't always a cheap way to get by. As well as slip rents, there are hull insurance and the burdens of short-term boat loans as compared to long-term house mortgages. Add to these the special expenses involved with boats—you don't have to haul out a house twice a year to paint its bottom. Liveaboards do enjoy many of the same benefits as homeowners, such as home/office income tax deductions, waiving capital gains taxes against the purchase of a boat that will be used as a residence, applying homeowners' tax exemptions to property taxes.

The actual monthly cost of living on a boat depends on the boat and the expectations of the people and their income. I asked a number of liveaboards in different parts of the country about their expenses to give you an idea of the national range. You can consider this sort of a geography lesson, and remember that the figures were gathered in 1976.

California

Marina del Rey. A couple on a 32-foot trawler say their costs are about equal to homeowners in the area. Slip rent is $110 a month; insurance, $410 a year; maintenance, about $50 a month. They figure they pay about $190 less than they did when they paid property taxes on the house they owned.

Newport Beach. A couple on a 32-foot cutter are at a mooring, so they pay only $192 a year. In the same place, a family on a 40-footer pay $165 a month for a slip at a marina.

Connecticut

Branford. A young couple on a 36-footer spend much of their time cruising. They figure their total expenses at dock (including food) run $480 a month at a marina. While cruising, expenses are cut more than half—to $200 a month.

Mystic. A man on a 38-foot cruiser says his slip rental and electricity come to about $900 a year. Add taxes and insurance and he still pays about 75 to 80 percent of what he would on land.

Old Greenwich. This is a high-priced commuter suburb of New York, and a couple on an old 70-foot cruiser say their slip runs $200 a month. Monthly charge for electricity is $15; for insurance, $100; for fuel and hot water, $20.

Stamford. Another expensive commuter-belt town. A couple living with their child on a 50-footer say their summer rate is $23 a foot; winter rate, $8 a foot. It averages out to about $175 a month, which is half the rent of an apartment in the area.

Florida

Marathon. Down in the Florida Keys, a retired couple on a 53-foot wooden Chris-Craft answer the cost question this way: "We'll have to make two answers. Is the question, 'How much does it cost?' or 'How much do we spend?' Our slip rental for the boat including electricity and water is about one hundred and sixty-five dollars a month. Now that's what it costs. But we have a telephone aboard which is extra. We have cable television which is extra. We haul our boat twice a year and this averages out to fifteen hundred dollars a year. We eat out quite a bit, mostly lunch, which we might or might not do living ashore. Our car expenses are greater, I believe, because we have no garage and the salt air is murder on anything metal. All this gets around to the question, 'How much do you spend?' We average about fifteen hundred dollars a month. Of course, things like groceries, clothes, transportation come close to being the same as on shore. Too, it doesn't have to cost this much, but we could easily spend more. I wouldn't want to try to discourage anyone contemplating living aboard. On the other hand, boat maintenance is expensive and getting more so all the time. I do a lot of my own work. A boat is not 'just like a house,' though people delude themselves into thinking it can be."

Miami. A family on a 43-foot yawl at Dinner Key Marina pay $51 a month, very reasonable as it includes electricity and water. However, they were awaiting an increase of 100 percent—maybe 300 percent!

Merritt Island. A young couple on a 30-footer figure their costs at $400 to $500 a month: "About twice as much as living ashore."

St. Petersburg. A family on a 45-foot Columbia pay $120 a month in the municipal marina. Electricity is metered and water included.

Venice. A retired couple who live well on their 38-foot ketch spend about $11,000 a year for everything, including food and hospitalization insurance. Boat expenses run $120 a month for the slip and electricity, $52 for insurance, $8 for diesel fuel.

Iowa

Sioux City. A young fellow on a 47-foot houseboat pays about $65 a month for his slip, "Much lower than land costs."

Louisiana

New Orleans. An older couple on a 27-foot sailboat pay about $65 for a slip through June, July, and August each year: "A super bargain which can't last."

Michigan

Saginaw. The boat is a 38-foot ketch and the couple who own her keep her at a do-it-yourself boatyard where the yearly cost is about $360. Big advantage of this type of yard: no requirements that the yard do the maintenance work.

New Jersey

Hightstown. The owner of a 56-foot wood cruiser says: "I pay by the foot, so my slip costs about twelve hundred dollars a year. In summer, electricity runs seventy dollars for six months. In the winter, the liveaboards assume the cost of all electricity in the marina, which comes to about forty to fifty dollars a month for me. If I add my boat payments, it comes to two thousand nine hundred and forty dollars a year, compared to the two thousand six hundred and forty dollars a year when I had a two-hundred-dollar-a-month apartment. For a difference of three hundred dollars, I have far more beauty and companionship here in the marina."

Mantoloking. Keeping a 40-foot trawler in this resort community runs about $700 a year for a slip, plus $500 a year for electricity (though this includes heating and cooking costs). The couple on board say it compares favorably to their landbound costs. At a house, they paid $500 a year for heat and $20 to $30 a month for electricity.

New York

Rochester. A couple on a 31-foot sailboat pay $60 a month for a slip plus $10 a month for electricity. In the same area, a one-bedroom apartment rents for about $250.

Rhode Island

Wickford. A couple on a 40-foot cruiser tell me: "We kept very careful, detailed records of costs this past year and found we lived comfortably on a budget of $900 a month, which is equivalent to our land costs. We ended our first eight months with a $700 saving, despite spending two months at a motel while a new engine was installed. We feel you can live more reasonably aboard than on shore with care. For one thing, our phone bill is lower."

Virginia

Norfolk. Just before taking off on a long-awaited cruise, a couple living on a 41-foot sailboat told me that they were paying $75 a month plus $10 for electricity: "We found that during the coldest months, two dollars' worth of charcoal a week kept us warm."

Washington

Port Angeles. A family on a 66-foot motor yacht pay $66 a month for a slip. Boat payments and insurance bring their monthly costs up to $800. They admit that their old house cost them about 40 percent of their present expenses, but "in ten years instead of thirty years, the boat will be paid for and the figures reversed."

At present living aboard in the States, unless you're cruising from place to place and hooking it, is getting expensive, especially when you have to figure in the costs of financing your boat. It's highest in resort areas and near the big cities. If you want to live at a dock at budget rates, try the backwaters. Or find a house with a private dock—there are a lot of these in California and Florida—and rent the dock from the owner. Some communities have called this a violation of zoning laws because, technically, a one-family house is being turned into a two-family unit. But it's tough to police this kind of situation.

Frankly, it's also tough to police harbors that have restrictions on hooking it for, say, more than 48 or 72 hours in one week. Privately, a member of the harbor patrol in San Francisco told me that with well over 700 boats in the harbor, it's difficult to enforce the 72-hour limit. He is well aware that there are live-aboards there who are quietly flouting the law.

9.

UMBILICAL CORDS

Face squarely up to it: You can't leave it all behind. When you move aboard and go cruising, you do escape mowing the lawn and shuck a lot of furniture that has to be dusted, but some things will always tie you to land. The binding cords can be as welcome as Christmas cards from friends that reach you in the Solomons, or as distasteful as the necessity of balancing a checkbook at long distance.

Mail

Ah, but you're staying put at a marina. Surely mail delivery will proceed just as it did at the house. Well, some marinas are very conscientious about mail, maintaining separate mailboxes for liveaboards or even delivering it to the boat. Other marinas toss the day's batch onto a table and let you sort it out. If the latter is the case, at least *insist* that incoming checks, packages, and magazines be held in the office—otherwise, they may disappear into someone else's pocket.

A better alternative if your mail is handled haphazardly is to pay a few extra dollars to rent a post office box, a decided advantage if you like to cruise when the whim hits and don't want to worry about mail piling up at the marina. (You can also request the post office to hold your mail, but this gets complicated if your cruising tends to be in small scattered chunks.) In popular boating centers, some liveaboards discovered that all the post office boxes were booked solid, so they hit on another solution—a telephone answering service. You can kill two birds with one stone this way, for the service will hold your mail and also take telephone messages at one depot.

Extended cruising is a whole different situation and there's probably no satisfactory way of handling mail. Trying to set up a firm itinerary takes the spontaneity out of cruising. I asked a number of cruising people what they did and the answers varied widely. Some use *poste restante* (the foreign equivalent of General Delivery); it's reliable in developed countries only. Others rely on harbor masters, foreign yacht clubs, and marinas, with good to indifferent results. One circumnavigator says he's found only two yacht clubs, one in Gibraltar and one in Palma de Mallorca, that are efficient about mail, and there's little point to mentioning their names because the situation changes so rapidly.

A very reliable system is American Express, which holds mail as a service to customers (you may be asked to produce an Amex card or Amex traveler's checks). The one drawback can be a long taxi ride in some ports to the Amex office. Also remember that Amex will hold mail only 30 days, after which it's returned to the sender. A fellow who's cruised extensively in his Garden-designed ketch gave me this thoughtful analysis:

"Amex is in business and appears to work harder to perform a service. *Poste restante* puts the burden on you, though it probably improves your chances of meeting interesting people in a port! Yacht clubs have been the least satisfactory for me, probably because they have more important agendas of their own and they rapidly tire of being bugged by transients. One of the best ways of alienating yourself from the club management is to keep harping on the mail that hasn't arrived, or putting them on the defensive about their service."

If you're cruising American ports, always tell friends to mark your mail "hold for delivery" when they send it care of General Delivery. One fellow reached Gloucester, Massachusetts, after a long passage up from the Islands and found all his accumulated mail had been returned after ten days. The powers that be at the post office tell me it will be held for 30 days if marked "hold for delivery"; ten days otherwise.

Package Delivery

Always use air freight overseas. It costs more, but the wait will be a week or two at most, not months as can happen with surface mail. Even air freight can be delayed overseas. One cruiser was stalled in Providenciales, Turks and Caicos Islands, for two weeks waiting for a shipment of hardware to arrive.

Make certain any replacement parts, sails, equipment, and so forth is consigned to the *yacht* and marked "ship's stores in transit." There's a fine legal point here. Your yacht is a little piece of America broken loose, so to speak, from the continent. Any goods in the form of ship's stores consigned to it (e.g.: *Yacht Maria*) can clear customs *without* duty. If the packages aren't properly marked, you can wind up paying a heavy duty on your new sail to get possession of it, then face a mountain of red tape trying to recoup your unnecessary expenditure.

One couple cruising in Europe told me they pulled a sneaky feat when they really needed an engine part in a hurry: They advised the shipper to mark the parcel "emergency medical supplies." The part arrived in a rush and went through customs. At this point, the couple innocently told the customs inspector that the parcel must have been marked wrong.

Finances

Handling your money while cruising is incredibly easier these days with communications shrinking the world. The smallest Mexican village can be just a Telex away from needed bank funds. However, for the sake of convenience, think of the ports you're hitting in relation to the type of credit or money you can use there. The big urban areas present few problems: Traveler's checks, credit cards (like Amex or BankAmericard), letters of credit, all are negotiable fairly easily. Smaller towns, as long as they have banking facilities, will exchange dollars or traveler's checks for the local currency. In the real backwaters, depend on local currency and dollars. As a rule of thumb, a cruising couple should keep about $200 in cash on board and about $500 in traveler's checks ($20 denomination preferably). Some people advise carrying a letter of credit. Frankly, these days, I think it can be a tremendous waste of time and energy. In an emergency, you can generally cash a personal check at a foreign bank, allowing about a week for clearance. I've arranged faster clearance simply by paying the cost of a telegram or long-distance call to my bank.

If you're dependent on a fixed monthly income in the form of a pension, social security, or a trust fund, you may want to have the checks deposited directly into your bank account. This is an easy system to set up; just talk to your banker before setting off on your cruise. A couple who've been cruising for quite a while did tell me that their pension and social security checks are mailed directly to them each month: "With the exception of Bermuda, they've reached us on time in over fifty countries on five continents." They've always had their checks mailed care of American Express or Thomas Cook, never *poste restante*.

About credit cards. In urban areas, the bank cards are in fairly wide circulation, but the best all-purpose card—almost an international form of money—is American Express or its British equivalent, Thomas Cook. The Amex card also lets you cash personal checks within limits at all their offices abroad (a full list of the outposts is in the 190-page Amex booklet "Services and Offices").

The one disadvantage to credit cards is that the bills pile up at home and dunning letters start coming in. If you don't have a reliable relative to handle these things, arrange to have your bank pay out the money. For emergencies, you can even leave your savings book with a bank and have them debit your account for any money sent you.

Telephone

Having your own telephone on a boat in a marina used to be a haphazard affair, with the wire strung from the dock, draped across the deck, and led through a hatch or opening port. Connections were poor because the telephone company originally used the same connecting elements it used on land, and these were corroded by salt spray and the elements.

So, Ma Bell asked Harvey Hubbell (the firm that makes electrical plugs, outlets, and cords for marine use) to come up with some good corrosion-resistant connections and they did. There's a marina outlet that connects with the telephone lines, a boat hull inlet that can be mounted almost anywhere, and a connecting vinyl cord that won't mar the boat's deck.

You can buy the Hubbell connectors yourself (using your builder's discount if you have one) and save about 40 percent on what Ma Bell charges. However, a couple with a schooner in Oceanside, California, tried to do just that, and they were told by the telephone company that the connection wouldn't be made unless they bought the components from Ma Bell. Price was $60 for the installation, and they would have to drill the hole for the hull inlet.

If you can't or won't have a telephone on board, it makes sense to get a telephone credit card. It makes long-distance calling easier and eliminates the scramble for change when you want to place a call.

You can use the card also for calls made ship-to-shore via your ship's radio, which is considered a very worthwhile investment at about $300 or so. This service is usually pretty good in America, though there is an extra charge of a buck or so for the trouble of hooking you into the land-based telephone network.

10.

HOMESTEADING THE OCEAN

The idea of living off the land, romanticized and given legitimacy by dozens of books and periodicals, including the one that really gave it national impact—the *Whole Earth Catalog*—can be amended to read "living off the sea." Some of the same resources used by subsistence livers on land, in fact, have always paid attention to the self-sufficient cruiser. A recent edition of the *Mother Earth News* put aside a fair amount of editorial space to talk about a couple who have been cruising the Caribbean, on a subsistence level, in a small sailing canoe. The same issue carried details on sprouting seeds, selling crafts, and other pursuits that are as useful to the couple on a home-built ketch as to the couple making a living off a five-acre homestead.

Maybe the most important resource right now for cruisers is the little magazine called *Windvane*, started by Jim Brown and his wife, Jo Anna, with the help of friends. It's written, edited, and published by cruising sailors interested in furthering the idea of self-sufficiency afloat. One issue had articles on carrying legal cargo, treating burns at sea, home preservation of fish, and how cleaning bottoms on a free-lance basis can help add some money to the strongbox. It's no-nonsense stuff, and it's all been tried and found to work. *Windvane* is a quarterly, runs about $5 a year, and is headquartered at 241 K West 35th Street, National City, California 92050.

Scattered ideas are available in the *Whole Earth Catalog*, the *Mother Earth News* (Box 70, Hendersonville, North Carolina 28739), the *Mariner's Catalogs* (really excellent stuff; International Marine Publishing, Camden, Maine 04843), the journal *Spray* put out by the Slocum Society (Box 857, Hilo, Hawaii 96720), and the journal of the Seven Seas Cruising Association (Box 38, Placida, Florida 33946).

The real bottom line for anyone who tries self-sufficiency is simply: "You gotta eat." All the chatter about chartering, trading cargo, and making jewelry from shells is no good unless the larder's full. If you're used to dropping in at the supermarket for your food, you'll be unprepared for the amount of time you need to spend just getting food from the sea and the shores. You're no longer just the "eater," you're also catcher, grower, processor, preserver, cooker.

You may not even want to eat some of the stuff that's free. Sea purslane, coon oysters, whelk, sea lettuce. The sort of thing you used to crumble underfoot on your beach walks. The fact is the stuff not only is free but also tastes good, and after you read one book, you'll want to go out and try it.

The book is Euell Gibbons's *Stalking the Blue-Eyed Scallop*, published by David McKay for about $2.95 paperback. Gibbons has a way of making all those distasteful things, like sour sorrel, sound like filet mignon, only better. He's amazed, and you'll be, too, that Americans reject so much that's readily available to any beachcomber. But as he says, maybe it's for the best. When Americans find out how delicious these freebies are, they'll be rare and expensive instead of free and plentiful.

A similar book is *The Edible Sea*, written by Paul and Mavis Hill, published by Barnes at $15. It tells you what kind of seaweed you can eat, how to harvest it, and even what to do with it (Krazy Kelp Kandy, for one). And the Hills talk about fish, mollusks, and reptiles as well. There's a section on food poisoning that every tropics cruiser should read.

Don't overlook the dangers of salmonella, a bacteria-induced disease with flu-like symptoms that comes from careless handling of fresh meats and other foods. The main problem on boats seems to be the chopping board and counters, which should be kept sanitized with boiling water after use.

When you think of getting your own food while cruising, you think of fishing from the sea. More about that in a moment. First, consider that you can also farm on board. I've come across a few cruising boats with pots of tomato plants, herbs, and lettuce's growing, like a floating farm, and the drawbacks of extra weight and occasional dirt spills on the deck are offset by the advantage of having a fresh salad with dinner.

There's another kind of on-board farming even more suitable for boats, and in fact the stuff you grow will have more vitamins than the food sold in supermarkets. It's called sprouting and all you need for it are seeds and some containers. You may have tried sprouting already if you're interested in health foods. Sprouts have no chemical preservatives to mess up the system and they pack the neat trick of developing more nutritional value than is in the seeds they grow from.

If you're really blank on the subject, here's some reassurance: You've no doubt eaten sprouts. Bean sprouts, for instance, are commonly used in Chinese cuisine. You can get similar tender sprouts from just about any seed, with exceptions like tomato and potato whose sprouts are toxic. Of course, you don't start with just any kind of seed, for the ones intended for planting are sometimes treated with insecticides. Maybe the safest way is to use seeds intended for sprouting as sold in health-food stores. You'll find varieties like alfalfa, corn, oat, wheat, mung bean, flax, and chia.

Next problem is keeping the seeds dry—and unsprouted—until you're ready to use them. Any large plastic containers with secure lids will do, though you might want the added protection of sealing the seeds inside a plastic bag before storing them in the containers.

Now all you need is a glass jar or one of those plastic margarine containers. Put a couple of teaspoons of seeds in the jar, cover with water, and let them soak a few hours. Then drain off the water and put a lid on the jar, first putting a couple of vent holes in the top with your ice pick. The basic idea in sprouting is to keep the seeds in a moist, dark place, perhaps a locker. Keep them moist by rinsing and draining them twice a day. In about three to five days, you'll have a jar full of sprouts.

Alfalfa seeds: Three tablespoons will yield a quart of sprouts in about three days. The best length for eating is about an inch.

Mung beans: Three-fourths cup yields a quart in three to four days. Best length, two to three inches.

Wheat: A cup of seeds will yield a quart of sprouts in about two days. Eat them when the sprout is about as long as the seed, one-fourth to one-half inch. Grasses like wheat, corn, and barley shouldn't be allowed to grow too long as they get tough and inedible.

Lentils: As with mung beans, you need three-fourths cup to get a quart. Growth takes two days and the best length is between one-half and one inch.

Sunflower seeds: You'll need about a cup of these big seeds to get a quart of sprouts. Keep them going for two days and eat them when the sprouts are about one-half-inch long.

You have to use the sprouted seeds right away unless you refrigerate them to stop the growing process. Cruising people who use sprouts start a kind of crop rotation system, beginning a small batch of seeds each day so that there's a fresh crop every dinner. What do you do with them? You can use them as a salad in place of lettuce, on sandwiches, in canned soups, as vegetables. You can blanch them with boiling water, then season, or you can fry them in oil for a minute or two.

Real farming—dirt farming—as we indicated raises some problems. Use potting soil rather than plain garden-variety dirt. The potting soil is lighter and disease-resistant. You can also cut weight by using plastic or styrofoam pots. The yields aren't great. The big pluses, as with sprouts, are having fresh food available on long cruises and the psychological boost of doing something that's nutritionally and ecologically better than

Tomato plant garden aboard a big liveaboard power cruiser.

opening a can. A book to read if you're interested is *Farming in a Flowerpot* by Alice Skelsey. It's about $3 from Workman Publishing, 231 East 51st Street, New York, New York 10022.

Living off land plants is often risky, sometimes parasitical, since most trees on islands are owned. Two exceptions are papaya and coconut that grow wild quite well. (Some trees have to be domesticated or else they're choked by the jungle or their fruit simply becomes inedible—oranges and pineapples being examples.) You can find coconuts on uninhabited islands as well as on the rim of civilization. Just hack them open with a small hatchet or hole the eyes to drain the milk. Ripe coconuts have a sloshy sound when you shake them. Younger ones have meat that isn't quite firm and may make you diarrhetic if you drink the milk.

You can tell a ripe papaya by its orange color. Scoop out the seeds and eat the fruit like a cantaloupe. Unripe papaya, light green but not yet yellow, can be treated almost like a vegetable (the way plantains are) and sautéed until tender.

When you get past these "acceptable" foods, you find a lot of stuff growing wild that no one on land would think to be bothered with. Yucca flowers, for example. They grow all over Florida and the crisp white petals make tasty additions to the salad bowl. Try the sweet red fruit of the prickly pear cactus (eat the pulp only), dark purple sea grapes, the small red/ yellow or purple coco plums that grow wild near the water, the green seed pods of the jumbie-bean shrub tree, which you boil until they're tender (roast and grind them and you have a reasonable substitute for coffee beans). In the tropics, look for the potatolike root called taro. You can mash it, or slice and fry it, and the tops taste a bit like spinach. The outside may give you the shudders—it's sort of scraggly looking—but peel it away and the innards will remind you of sweet potato.

In the South Seas, try breadfruit, literally the bread of these islands. Bake it in its own skin until black on each side, hack it open and you have dinner. It's all the better if you build the fire on a beach.

The shores hold living things, too, that you'll want for your larder. Go clamming or spend an afternoon prying oysters off rocks. What you'll eat will be nothing like the stuff that comes in cans.

Fish will be naturally one of the important parts of your diet if you are into living on a subsistence level. The only problem is staying abreast of local laws wherever you are. Spearfishing, for example, was prohibited in the Bahamas at this writing and poachers could have their boats confiscated. Out at sea, you're on your own, free of licensing, legal limits, and the like. All you need is some heavy line, lures, and hooks (fancy rods and reels are unnecessary). You might want to add a gaff, handy on high-sided sailboats, but remember to keep the hook protected with a cork when it's stowed. Use 60-pound test line or better, and really heavy line if you're going after big ones. If you take rods along, put some PVC tubes overhead to stow them in so they don't tangle with you and your hair, and secure them with a safety line to the boat when you're "trolling"; otherwise, you can lose them overboard.

If you get a good catch, you'll have more fish on your hands than you can use at a single meal, so think about preserving it. We're assuming you don't have the luxury of a freezer at your disposal—as you'll see, you can manage very well without this expensive piece of consumption. You have a few choices: canning, which requires special equipment, or the simpler methods of smoking, corning, drying, and brine-salting.

Just a few words on what preservation is all about. Basically, you're protecting the fish from the bacteria that cause it to rot. The bacteria need warmth and humidity to grow, so your aim is to remove moisture from the fish and store it at a temperature that the bacteria don't like. Keep cured fish products below 70 degrees if you want the maximum shelf life. Cured fish can also be affected by chemical spoilage (oxidation when the surface of the fish is allowed to hit the air or sunlight) and physical spoilage (damage by insects, cockroaches, and rats). To protect your cured fish from these dangers, you also want to keep them in tightly closed containers (brine-cured products should be kept under the surface of the brine).

Corning

This is really a temporary method that will hold fish for about 24 hours, a bit longer in cooler temperatures. It's one that sportsfishermen use when they're far from home, the weather's warm, and there isn't adequate refrigeration. Simply bleed the fish by pulling out the gills and wash it as soon as possible after catching it. Make a mixture of about a tablespoon of pepper to a cup of salt for up to 2 pounds of fish and rub this in the belly cavity and over the skin. Then put the fish in a container with a few layers of burlap draped over it, but not touching the fish.

Keep the burlap damp. Before you cook the fish, rinse it well—and don't add salt!

Brine-Salting

This is a sophisticated version of salting, and it's the method used to salt herring as you've probably come across it in Scandinavian cooking. A two-gallon crock with a tight-fitting lid is ideal, but glass, plastic, stainless-steel, and enamel containers are almost as good. You also need a lot of salt. Some people prefer the coarse-grained salt used by commercial houses, but actually fine-grained salt forms into brine and penetrates the fish quicker.

Clean and fillet the fish, put a layer of salt on the bottom of the crock, then layer the fish alternately with layers of salt. Probably it's a good idea to dredge the fish in salt before you layer in order to work salt into any scorings.

"Lean" fish work better than "fat" fish, simply because they're easier for the salt to penetrate. Saltwater fish that work well with this method are bluefish, cod, hake, pollack, sea trout, channel bass, striped bass, salmon, shad, rockfish, mackerel, herring, and Florida mullet.

Once you have the fish layered with salt, they'll start forming their own brine. Make sure the fish are weighted down (maybe with a pot lid) so the brine will cover them.

Small fish up to 8 pounds will cure in about two days, but, generally, larger fish take a week to ten days. Then repack the fish in fresh salt and stow away: They should last up to nine months, even longer. But remember to rinse the fish and soak them in two or three changes of water over several hours before using them.

Drying

This is a great method for subsistence sailors because it requires no equipment, doesn't deplete your salt supply, and gives you a supply of fish for soup and stews. All you do is clean and fillet the fish, cut it into thin pieces, and hang the strips out in a hot sun (a few knots of wind helps the drying process) with thread or thin wire. A day out should give the fillets a good protective coating, with the insides able to dry more slowly. You'll want to bring the strips in at night, I'm afraid, letting them drape around the cabin. They can't be exposed to dew. When the fish is completely dry, it will keep for a couple of months.

Smoking

This is a super method as far as taste goes, but it's difficult unless you can get your hands on a true smoker (one that smokes and preserves the fish, not one that cooks it as well) or can improvise a smoker with the chimney from your wood stove, should you have one. Obviously, this last isn't a method for the tropics. Basically, what you would have to do is trap the smoke in a box of some kind with a flap to regulate the flow of smoke. Hang the fillets in the smoke by looping string over a stick resting on top of the box. The filleted fish should first be soaked in brine (three to ten hours, depending on size) then dried.

The fire should be smothered with green wood so that you get a good bit of smoke. How long you smoke is up to your taste buds, but the longer you do it, the longer the fish will be preserved, up to several months. You should smoke for at least a day, but this can be really unwieldy on a boat. You may want to build a makeshift smoker on the beach instead.

Canning

You need a pressure cooker for canning on board; it's the only way you can get the fish (or meat, fruit, and vegetables) up to a high enough temperature for safe canning. (Fruit and acid vegetables can be done safely in boiling water in an open pan, but don't try this with fish.) You fill a pint-size, self-sealing Kerr or Mason jar with fish, leaving about an inch of space at the top (a can sealer is a nice luxury if you can afford $50 and the space to stow it); add a teaspoon of salt, tighten the lid, and place the jar in the pressure cooker with water to a depth of two-thirds the height of the jar. When the water boils, adjust the cooker's lid and cook for about an hour and 45 minutes at ten pounds' pressure. You can get a pressure gauge (and canning instructions) from National Presto Industries, Eau Claire, Wisconsin 54701.

Catching, growing, and preserving your own food can give you the satisfaction of a simple existence, a basic one, free of the hassles of working at any job in order to fill the larder. You're basically operating in a very natural way. How unnatural it all seems to work nine to five in an office or a factory in order to buy canned vegetables and old fish, when you can spread your table with fresh foods gotten by your own labor.

Part IV.
Preparation for
Adventure

11.

AS BASIC AS
FOOD AND WATER

A word about stowing your food and all other supplies on the boat. A 40-foot boat loaded to the planking with supplies for a long cruise gets to seem roughly 140 feet when the time comes to find something. God knows, lists aren't fun, but they save aggravation and short tempers on long cruises. Make an inventory as you load the boat.

You'll want two things. First, make a layout chart with every locker and stowage area on the boat given a number. Second, make an alphabetized list of everything you take on. Not just cans of potatoes and green beans, but repair parts for the engine, oil, spare bilge pump—everything. Mark next to each item the number of the stowage area where you've put it.

There are two systems for loading cans and other food on boats. Some people find it simple to pack everything by preordained meal plans—all the stuff for one meal in one place. Some find this hopelessly systematized under way. On one Atlantic crossing, the crew tried the prearranged menu bit but rearranged everything a week out by variety of contents—all the meats in one area, vegetables in another, fruit in another. Said the skipper, "Prearranged menus seem to work best on single-handed or two-person boats. With five in our crew, we really preferred the option of deciding each day what we wanted and switching around as we liked. It's less regimented that way."

There are other hazards in stocking a boat. Bring aboard food, and you worry about roaches, rats, mold, rusted cans, bacteria. But maybe the biggest hazard of all is the contamination of the taste buds—simple boredom—that afflicts boats whose neophyte owners worry more about shelf life than the joy of eating. When one highly ballyhooed circumnavigation was aborted last year in the Caribbean, the female half of the team said it was bland food as much as bad weather that prompted her decision to go home. A young crewman said about the stores on a 41-foot sloop on which he crossed the Atlantic:

"The first thing I saw when I met the boat in the Chesapeake were the cans. A mountain of cans was sitting on the dock next to her and the owner and his wife were stripping off labels, varnishing, and marking them. It must have been ninety degrees the next day and we spent the whole time marking cans—three of us—which gives you an idea how many cans there were. Anyway, if it was edible and can-able, we had it. The owner and his wife had this suburban hang-up about fresh food. They didn't bring any on board except for six dozen eggs that we ate like mad because they were fresh. There were no potatoes, fruit, or greenstuffs, just hundreds of cans of peaches, spaghetti, and green beans.

"If I had known, I would have brought more stuff with me, but we were in a really remote dock and I couldn't get any fresh food in the area—no car either. So I went with just a lot of nuts and sunflower seeds I had along. Incidentally, we also had backup supplies of fifty pounds of dried eggs and thirty pounds of powdered milk—ugh!

"Fortunately, the ocean provided us with flying fish—no line needed. The fish are attracted by the white sails during the night; you can hear them plunking against the cloth and thudding on the deck during the night. Next morning, you just collect them and sauté them with garlic and oil. Really tasty.

"We had two bad storms that made cooking almost impossible, and it was then that I missed something handy like dried fruits. You have to eat for the sake of eating during a storm and it was hell to come off watch to a cold can of ravioli.

"I came back with three strong food memories of that voyage: the cans of cold ravioli, the flying fish, and the popcorn. That's right. About two thousand miles out into the Atlantic, we remembered the bag of popcorn on board and cooked it. Every boat needs a surprise like that on a long voyage."

Now it may be that you have simple tastes. I've just heard, for instance, about an Englishman and a friend who sailed from Panama to Australia on a diet of eggs, potatoes, onions, and spaghetti. But generally, you'll want some surprises (a handful of nuts on a night watch becomes a rare treat) and some fresh food. You'll also want every kind of spice and herb you can fit in—dump them in plastic Zip-Loc bags and take them along.

Remember that going offshore, a cookbook may be more liability than help. Those glorious Julia Child or James Beard books have hundreds of recipes that won't do you any good at all in the doldrums when you can't get fresh cream. What you need is some imagination about what to do with a can of mushrooms. Onions and herbs are probably the most useful things you'll have in the galley, because some sautéed onions or a pinch of rosemary can make all the difference in the world to a can of beef stew.

What Travels?

The more fresh foods you can take, the better. They come in their own wrapping (no cans to dispose of) and what you bring with you, you have. While cruising, much of your time will be spent in ports where fresh food is available, though it can be expensive in places like Bermuda and some Caribbean islands where much of it is imported. In some out-of-the-way areas, fresh foods may be unavailable. There are Pacific islands where villagers may scarcely have enough eggs for their own consumption.

A number of people cruise long-distance without refrigeration and they do it quite happily. The ice chest on one friend's boat hasn't seen any ice in three years, with no one succumbing to scurvy or other foul diseases. Refrigeration easily becomes a thing you can do without, along with TV and tub baths. (The only things you really need on a boat are a good book and a jug of wine.) Anyway, you soon learn which fresh foods travel *well*.

Eggs, for instance. They're versatile, protein-rich, and you can take them with you. The trick is to buy them as fresh as possible (this goes for all fresh foods), from a farmer if you can, and before the eggs are washed and chilled. Then rub each egg with petroleum jelly and store them in styrofoam cartons—not cardboard ones. By the way, don't toss the cartons away when they're empty as you won't find them in native markets and they're the greatest cure for breakage since the invention of the eggshell. Eggs should last for four to five weeks if you follow these precautions. And that's enough to get you to Europe.

Cheeses sealed in wax, like Gouda and Bonbel, have a long storage life provided you keep them as cool as possible by storing them in the bilge. Some people prevent mold from taking hold in cut cheese by wrapping the cut section in vinegar-soaked cloth. Effective if you like the taste of vinegar.

Potatoes and onions will last for well over a month if well ventilated. Oranges, grapefruit, limes, and lemons will also stay fresh for weeks if you wrap them individually in aluminum foil and keep them in cool lockers close to or below the waterline. Go through any wrapped stocks every week and discard anything that's starting to go bad.

Some foods you can buy when they're still green, letting them ripen on board so you have a little harvest just when the canned goods are starting to pall. Buy avocados as rock hard as possible, and very green bananas and tomatoes.

Cured country ham and bacon, the kind you see advertised through mail-order houses, will last indefinitely. Just cut off a slab when you need it and rewrap in the muslin bag.

Pumpkins, parsnips, eggplants, radishes, and currants will

last a week or two on board. Squash, cabbage, sweet potatoes should last a month.

Lettuce is a poor traveler, but it will last up to a week if you buy tightly packed heads and keep them in a cool locker. Incidentally, if you're taking leafy green vegetables aboard that you've bought in a native market, and worry they may contain bugs, dunk them in a bucket of salt water for about ten minutes. The bugs will crawl out and drown.

Cans—The Inevitable

Other than the joys of playing Russian roulette with the menu should the labels peel off, there's a reason for taking paper labels off cans and marking them by contents. Damp labels lead to rust that leads to little pinprick holes through which bacteria can enter. The bacteria danger is greater if the cans are sloshing around in bilge water rather then in dry lockers. Acidic foods like fruits and tomato sauce are least susceptible to bacteria, so unless the rust is excessive, they should be edible.

Another problem that crops up with cans is a kind of discoloration of the tin. This happens when an acidic food (say spaghetti in tomato sauce) eats through the tin coating. A slight discoloration is harmless and just indicates that the food may have a metallic taste. If the "detinning" has gone too far, the cans will start to swell up—don't eat the contents.

Some protection from bilge water can be gotten by packing the cans in heavy-duty trash bags. These also help to buffer the cans a bit in stowage.

Some canned goods are hard to find outside the U.S.A., like small cans of boned chicken and large cans of turkey and pork. You won't have much trouble finding American goods in the Caribbean, but British and Danish products are often just as good and cheaper. The farther west you go into the Pacific, the more expensive the tinned foods become, and even fresh foods—recently, eggs were going for $2 a dozen in Tahiti. After American Samoa and Fiji, the prices really escalate. However, there are trade-offs: the wonderful cheap creamery butter in

New Zealand, the fresh exotic fruits of French Polynesia, and in the Atlantic the steaks of Argentina.

Dry Foods

You thought only old-time square-riggers got weevils. Shades of Horatio Hornblower tapping his biscuits on the table to chase the little buggers out. Unfortunately, modern boats get them, too. Things like noodles, spaghetti, and rice last about six months, while bread and cake mixes may last only three.

You can fumigate grains while stocking the boat, but it's a pesky process. You have to get dry ice, crush it and add a few tablespoons to all the storage containers you'll be using. Pour the grain over the ice and leave the container lids slightly ajar for about 30 minutes or until the vaporization of the carbon dioxide gas stops. Then seal. What's happened is that the oxygen in the container has been replaced by the gas; this retards oxygen spoilage and helps eliminate the pest problem.

Once you do get bugs, particularly roaches, on board, they're hard to get rid of. The most effective way is to use the professional-type bombs or foggers that give off a poisonous mist that permeates everywhere. You cover all the food and eating utensils, discharge a bomb, close up the boat, and leave for the day. Then ventilate the boat well before going back on board to stay, as the fumes are dangerous to humans, too. You'll find an army of dead roaches waiting for you, stiff as boards with feet in the air, and crackly as Rice Krispies when you step on them. Spray again in a couple of weeks to get the newly hatched roaches.

Freeze-Dried and Dehydrated Foods

Food is mostly water. Think about it and you may get irritated about all those heavy cans sloshing around in your bilges —80 to 90 percent of the weight is water. A number of cruising yachtsmen have found they can eliminate this excess weight by using freeze-dried or dehydrated foods, whose other great advantage is that neither type needs refrigeration. Contrary to common belief, the two types are not the same. The most important difference for the yachtsman is that freeze-dried foods have the same bulk as whole foods, so there's no space saving, whereas dehydrated foods shrink when the water is removed.

Craig Sallin who runs Family Reserve Foods in Fort Lauderdale, Florida, put this comparison table out on the two types for the benefit of the cruising boatmen who stock up at his store:

	Dehydrated	*Freeze-Dried*
Shelf Life		
Unopened Can	Indefinite (15+ years)	Indefinite (15+ years)
Opened Can	1 year with lid 3–4 months for milk and eggs.	2–3 weeks with lid, or rehydrate contents and freeze.
Bulk	Very compact. Product shrinks in dehydration process, expands when rehydrated.	Doesn't shrink at all. Size of original product is size of freeze-dried product. However, is lighter in weight.
Number of cans and cost to equal:		
20 lbs. corn	1 #10 can ($18.20)	2¼ #10 cans ($13.50)
20 lbs. green beans	1 #10 can ($13.50)	3½ #10 cans ($14.85)
8 dozen eggs	1 #10 can ($13.20)	3 #10 cans ($45.00)
Items Available	Everything except meat.	Premixed entrees, fruits, meats, vegetables, and eggs. No grains or dairy products.
Preservatives	Generally less than canned goods. Less than one-half the items have preservatives.	Almost none.

	Dehydrated	*Freeze-Dried*
Nutrition	Good. Vitamins remain in food rather than in water as in canned goods.	Excellent.
Preparation	Rehydrate in cold water or cook if appropriate.	Add boiling water; cold water for some items.
Flavor	Comparable to frozen.	Most like fresh.
Size of containers	#2½ and #10 cans	#10 cans; also foil pouches.
Cost of year's supply per person	About $395	About $1,500
Space requirements	About one-fifth the space of can stowage.	About equal to conventional can stowage.

There are several sources for dehydrated and freeze-dried foods. Family Reserve, the one we mentioned, is at 4718 N.E. 12th Avenue, Ft. Lauderdale, Florida 33308. My only quibble with freeze-dried foods is the ice cream—definitely to be avoided. It looks like cellulose sponge when you add water.

Do buy the #10 cans; anything smaller is too expensive space-wise and price-wise. Remember, too, to get a supply of plastic lids to reseal the cans. You can usually get them from your supplier, or recycle the lids from containers for margarine.

Supplementing Supplies Abroad

Practice some discrimination and common sense when aboard. You wouldn't think (I hope) of tramping into a farmer's field in Maryland or Nebraska and gathering up an armful of corn or tomatoes. Don't do it to the natives in the

Pacific where most island land is privately owned. That beautiful stand of banana trees probably belongs to someone—it's his livelihood. Imagine how he feels walking down to the shoreline and seeing the bananas he's carefully planted and tended ripening by the stalk on your yacht anchored off.

By the same token, many cruising people who carry guns say they're useful in shooting small game on shore for the table. But make sure you're shooting *wild* game. There's the well-known story of the European crew who landed on a Pacific island and shot the village goats for their larder.

This kind of story is all the more shocking because every cruising yachtsman knows how incredibly generous villagers can be when you ask permission to buy some of their goods. Often their fruit ripens all at once in quantities they can't use, so they appreciate the extra revenue.

In remote areas, trading goods are more welcome than money when it comes to getting supplies like fresh bread, fruits, vegetables, and eggs. On most small Pacific islands, for instance, fish hooks, nylon fishing line, and sinkers are gratefully received. It pays to carry a locker of trading goods with you and you may want to make some advance preparations before you leave. A good source for those fishing stocks is a professional supply house called Nylon Net Co., 7 Vance Avenue, Box 592, Memphis, Tennessee 38101. For about $4, you can get a five-pound bag of egg sinkers or a thousand #6 Mustad hooks for your trading days.

What else is welcome?

Levi's (Clean ones, please; they're in demand almost everywhere.)
Small cans of paint
Costume jewelry (Don't discard your old stuff so fast; take it with you.)
Empty bottles
Magazines with plenty of good color photographs (Village schoolteachers are usually grateful to be given some of these, too.)

Toys (magnets, small cars with movable wheels, dolls, etc.)
Rope
Knives

You'll want to take things like these along as gifts as well as for trading. Quite often on your voyage, you'll be entertained and befriended by the locals, and it's good to reciprocate. But save the gifts until just before you leave; otherwise, you may be inundated with gifts in return by islanders who can ill afford their own matchless generosity.

Water

You never take fresh water for granted, even on a short cruise. Your water tanks should routinely receive a purifying agent at each filling in strange ports. And the procedure should be repeated for the emergency supplies kept in jerry cans. You can use one of the commercially available tablets or simple household Clorox, adding about a teaspoon of Clorox for ten gallons of water. If the water is cloudy or discolored, double the dosage.

Clorox kills bacteria, but not amoeba. Iodine will take care of both, and the rule is three quarts to 1,000 gallons of water. Or, if you add iodine until the taste and the color change a bit, that's enough.

Be careful—never pump water into your tanks overseas without tasting it first. Some unwary cruisers have pumped their 100-gallon tanks full of salt water before they realized this was what was being piped onto the docks where they were staying.

12.

KEEPING SHIPSHAPE

The problems of the world cruiser are a lot different from those of the weekend sailor who, lulled into a vague carelessness by the thought of nearby ports and repairmen, makes do with a pair of pliers and a screwdriver. The world cruiser, on the other hand, grimly faces the fact that he should be prepared to literally build his boat again with the tools and parts on board. It's not overly cautious to have spares for spares, and the truest luxury is backup or redundancy on critical points: VHF (very high frequency), single sideband, depthfinder.

Whatever you take, don't make the mistake of treating it offhandedly or you may end up with piles of rusted junk. Seal all the parts in waterproof containers. Check them and your tools periodically, keeping them well oiled. Metal toolboxes are just about useless on a boat. Either build-in a wooden chest with removable trays or buy a few wood or plastic toolboxes.

For General Repairs and Hull Repairs

A small clamp-on vise is really useful, especially if you can build a workbench into your boat (forward cabin, possibly) and keep it mounted in place. A really handy thing is the Zyliss

Lillian Welch is a 55-year-old accountant who had never done any carpentry work before moving aboard her 56-foot Elco, but she learned to handle all the routine maintenance. Here she's putting on a new deck.

Vise, imported from Switzerland by Westminster Export Co., 655 Highland Avenue, Atlanta, Georgia 30312. It does the work of a single vise and also serves as three gluing clamps (if you figure on doing woodwork), more than justifying the cost of about $80.

A small woodsaw and a hacksaw with extra blades can be useful not only for repairs, but also in emergencies—when the mast goes and you're left with a tangle of rigging. Only problem is that the blades can be really hard to keep in shape and rust-free. This is something you have to keep well-oiled.

Take along a good hand drill, with a supply of bits (and duplicates) from one-eighth inch to one inch. An electric drill, one that can be powered off the ship's 12V electrical system, is a nice luxury. A brace and bit are useful, though sometimes difficult to use in tight corners.

Claw hammer.

Three-pound sledge.

Tape measure—a six-footer is best.

Wood and cold chisels.

Small square with adjustable bevel.

Screwdrivers, both Phillips and common. Also, take along screwdriver bits for the drill.

For a wood-hulled boat, you'd want sheet plywood cut to stow under the bunk pads, both one-quarter inch and one-half inch. Include as much stowable hard wood pieces as you can handle. You'll want to have as large a supply of galvanized nails and spikes, and as many bronze, galvanized, and stainless-steel screws as possible. Include some very long galvanized bolts, about three-eighths inch. Finally, take along cotton batting and caulking compounds for working on seams.

For general use, tapered wooden plugs in various sizes.

For metal hulls, stow primer paint, double patches made up in a dozen sizes with a bolt through the middle of each, and an underwater patching compound such as Pettit's Polypoxy or Life-Calk.

For fiber-glass hulls, fiber-glass mat and cloth, patching compound, epoxy resin and polyester resin (activator).

For Rigging and Sail Repairs

Wire cutters capable of cutting the largest wire on the boat, and tested to make certain that it can indeed do this.

Some inexpensive galvanized turnbuckles, toggles, cotter pins, clevis pins, shackles, spare blocks, a length of galvanized wire at least equal in length to the longest stay, snap-shackles.

Bosun's chair.

Grommet tool, sailmaker's palm and needles (you can keep them rust-free by storing them in a jar filled with coffee grounds).

Rip-Stop tape, various weights of sail cloth, sail twine, sail slides and shackles, grommets, sail stops and battens in the necessary lengths.

For Plumbing Repairs

Wrenches. A tubing cutter, a flaring tool, and small wire cutters can also be useful.

Hose lengths, both plastic and rubber, along with plenty of spare hose clamps.

Nipples, adapters, reducers, and Teflon tape.

Spare parts for the head and pumps.

For Electrical Repairs

An inexpensive test meter (a $10 one should do nicely) and you'll want extralong test leads, more useful than the short test probes that the manufacturer provides. Buy a spare internal battery for the meter as well.

A multipurpose crimping tool, the kind that will also strip insulation, cut wire, and so forth. A stripper-cutter is probably also a good idea.

Fourteen-gauge copper wire (it solders easily) in the stranded and plastic-coated variety. If possible, buy more than one color of wire. Also, buy plastic P-clips to hold the wire in place.

A selection of crimp-on connectors and splices, plus any special terminals that may be used on your boat.

A 12V battery-powered soldering iron, if you can find one. Alternatives are tape solder, which can be melted by a match flame, and a miniature butane soldering iron, for which you would have to carry spare cylinders.

Vinyl insulating tape.

Clear silicone sealer.
Spare bulbs and fuses.
Battery lugs and cable.
Hydrometer for the battery.
Brushes for the starter motor, generator.
Spare starter motor.
Diodes for the alternator.
Spare switch or circuit breaker for your panel board.

For Engine Repairs

As well as the standard tools for general repairs, you'll want an adjustable open-end wrench large enough for the rudder post stuffing box.

For gasoline engines, carry a gasket set, rebuilding kit for the carburetor, coil distributor cap and rotor, points, condenser, ignition leads, spark plugs, water pump, fuel pump, belts, gasket cement, alternator, engine oil, transmission fluid, grease.

For diesel engines, add injectors, injector leads, filters, belts, and water-pump impellers.

An absolute must is a good repair manual for your engine, kept in a waterproof envelope. A half-decent mechanic can usually fix an engine he hasn't worked on before, as long as you can put the information in his hands.

If you can stand the expense, take along a spare propeller with an extra retaining nut, key, and pin.

Locating good tools is harder than you think. Some excellent sources for specialized shipbuilding tools are listed in the *Mariner's Catalogs* published by International Marine Publishing, Camden, Maine 04843. You should also get a catalog from the Brookstone Co. (122 Vose Farm Road, Peterborough, New Hampshire 03458). They specialize in some hard-to-find items like a good whetstone kit, professional quality tap and die sets, miniature welding torches.

If sails are the problem, a quick solution overseas may be to contact a used-sail broker in the States. Bacon and Associates (528 Second Street, Annapolis, Maryland 21403) keep an inventory of 3,000 to 4,000 sails on hand. In fact, you might want to talk to them before leaving the United States, as did the fellow who bought a secondhand set of sails for "work" so he could "dress up" when he entered foreign ports. Call (301-263-4880) or write for a carefully edited, mimeographed list of what they have in your range of requirements. There's even a list for boat awnings and gaff-headed sails.

Most of Bacon's sails are used, accepted for brokerage after a boat's been destroyed, rerigged, or reoutfitted for racing. They also get some new sails, surplus stock from dealers, and cancellations from sailmakers. The bargains can be considerable. How would you like a Hood Genoa, 54-foot luff in very good condition for $450? The "Low $$" list has the biggest bargains, though the sails may be in only fair shape.

If you're calling from a foreign port, Bacon urges you make arrangements in advance with customs to have the sails passed free of duty—the sails should be consigned directly to your yacht. Duty is presently 400 percent on sails in Argentina, for example. Payment by bank draft on a U.S. bank is preferred, but you can wire a deposit by cable. Personal checks are acceptable only on U.S. banks or their foreign branches. Shipments abroad are generally best sent air freight.

It's comforting to know that Bacon is a small company, run by people who know boats and their business from luff to batten pocket. Nobody is allowed to answer the phone unless he can also answer your questions intelligently, which is reassuring when you're searching your pockets for change in a phone booth.

A long-time cruiser offers this advice about that bane of the long-distance boatman—equipment failure: "You have to get out of the habit of thinking 'boatyard' only. In the Azores, we had our radio repaired by a serviceman at the U.S. base there. In New Guinea, friends with generator trouble went to a mining company and asked to talk to the chief engineer. He fixed it!"

Prices can be incredible. One cruiser was horrified to find alcohol priced at $12 a gallon at a remote outpost in the Pacific. He quickly switched to the more affordable kerosine. Had to buy a new stove, but he figured it was worth it.

Prices are what's behind the new interest in alternate power sources. Two things you might want to look into are solar power and wind-driven alternators.

At least four of the 1976 Observer Single-handed Transatlantic Race (OSTAR) boats crossed the Atlantic with silicon solar cell devices charging their batteries. The units are made by Solar Power Corp., 23 North Avenue, Wakefield, Massachusetts 01880, and because they also manufacture units for homes and industry, they should be around for a while—some companies in this field rise and fall overnight like mushrooms.

When I talked to the people at Solar Power, they had in the office the unit that *Third Turtle*, one of the OSTAR boats, carried mounted on her aft deck, and it was still in fine shape. It's an E-365 (about $300) and it puts out three amps for every five peak sunlight hours. The E-369 (about $600) puts out seven and one-half amps, they told me. One problem is that these units are not made with a protective shell, so you have to be careful not to step on them and damage the cells. Dick Newick, who designed *Third Turtle*, remarks: "A year ago, I would have called these things gadgets. Now, I call them necessities." He says his boat ran her running lights and Tillermaster off the batteries coming across and arrived with more battery charge than she had when she left England.

Another company in the field is Solar International, 636 Arleigh Rd., Severna Park, Maryland 21146. I spoke to a family that used five of their panels on their ketch during an 8,000-mile cruise. They found these very strong—you can step on them. Their advice, if you're buying solar panels, is to look for *no* exposed metal parts, *no* connections that have to be made on deck, impact protection (three-sixteenths-inch Lexan or plexiglas cover), and fiber-glass backing (not aluminum).

The Ampair 50 wind-driven alternator was tested on two 1976 OSTAR entries as well as on a cruising yawl that covered

The solar panel mounted on *Third Turtle*. Photograph by Steven Izenour.

12,000 miles with a prototype. It was specifically designed for mounting on the mast of a cruising yacht and produces up to 50 watts of 12V DC electricity, or enough to keep up a small auto-pilot or fluorescent cabin lights and charge the batteries. Weight is low, and because of the streamlined design so is windage. Imtra Corp., 151 Mystic Avenue, Medford, Massachusetts 02155.

13.

LONG-DISTANCE CRUISING:
SOME SCENARIOS AND SOLUTIONS

First, understand that cruising conditions change overnight, which is either a hassle or an adventure depending on how sanguine a disposition you have. Channels silt in, prices change (usually up), a friendly boatyard operator retires, civil unrest takes a whole country off your cruising itinerary.

For years, the small core of serious blue-water sailors have been keeping each other informed of what's happening by writing their own journals. Maybe the best known is *Flying Fish*, the publication of the British-based Ocean Cruising Club. (The OCC has strict membership requirements—belonging *is* an honor. You can find out more about it by writing the secretary at 33 Brickwall Close, Burnham-On-Crouch, Essex, England.)

An American group that does a similar, excellent job of reporting the cruising climate is the Seven Seas Cruising Association whose monthly *Commodores' Bulletin* covers everything from the price of water in Antigua to good anchorages in the New Hebrides.

The SSCA modestly calls itself a "voluntary dis-organization." It was started in 1952 in California by some cruising folk who wanted to share their experiences, and it's grown into a worldwide association of some of the best-known cruising sailors. It's a tightly knit group, those people who fly the red, white, and blue SSCA flag, and a select one in the best sense of the word. To be eligible, you have to live aboard a seagoing boat that is actively cruised, and you must be recommended by two current members. On this last point, the *Bulletin* puts it very well: "Commodores are cautioned to recommend only someone they know well and to ask themselves the question, 'Do I really want to follow in his wake along some foreign shore?' Any member who knowingly breaks the laws of a country or leaves unpaid bills in port may be dropped, and every member is expected to leave in port a feeling of welcome for those who come after."

The information contributed by members is a little astounding in its diversity and care. Do you want to know the price of bread in French Polynesia, the name of a reliable bar owner who will hold mail in the Azores, a boat boy in Singapore who will help paint your boat for $1.50 a day? It's probably in the *Bulletin,* and nonmembers of the SSCA can subscribe at $7 a year. The address: SSCA, Box 38, Placida, Florida 33946.

You learn by reading the cruising literature that the people doing it really enjoy the sights, sounds, flavors of foreign ports. The sea is a common denominator between them and the coastal people they meet. The fact that they've gone to the trouble of going to a land in a small boat endears them to the native population far more than arrival in a Boeing 747 or a bus.

There are irritations, of course. We're not saying that these things will happen to you, but they have happened to other people who went cruising.

1. Twilight off the coast of Indonesia. The five people on a big ketch spotted a couple of fishing boats approaching from shore. Just about the time one of the crew said it was a shame the light was too dim for photographs, the supposed fishermen opened fire. Pirates! Luckily for the the people on the ketch, it had a good engine and it caught right away, getting them out of trouble on that nearly windless night.

Katie Hamilton, who recently spent a year cruising with her husband, Gene, flops on deck while the vane steering does the work. "Best crewmember we had," she recalls.

A kind of small-time coastal piracy still exists. Like official corruption, it's a symptom of a splintered government that's lost control over its territory to some extent. A country torn by unrest or political division has difficulty policing its own capital, let alone its coastal waters.

Added to this small-time piracy is the danger of drug-trade hijackings. There have been some well-documented cases of private yachts being stolen and used to smuggle drugs through the Caribbean or Pacific. Even bulk marijuana can be loaded into a trash compactor (sales of these flourished a few years ago in the Islands) and baled for transport in yachts not built for carrying cargo.

For these reasons, a number of cruising boats carry guns. Much to the horror of, say, our British cousins who find it a barbarous extension of American violence. Certainly, guns may be acceptable practice in the U.S.A., but overseas governments are wary of aliens arriving with weapons, even if they're going to be used only for self-defense. Some countries will impound guns on arrival and return them to you on departure. They may even impound your very flare pistol. Other countries will just seize them and you may or may not get them back. It's better to declare your firearms and face the inconvenience of having them handled legally—it's better than jail or the loss of your boat.

2. The anchorage at Cumberland Bay in St. Vincent. A Connecticut man and his wife had come there to find peace, quiet, tranquillity. Instead they found noise, crowds, and pesky natives. "We ended up paying one character five bucks just to get him off our boat," the man told me. The problem is poverty compounded with a lack of naïveté. In the South Pacific, there are islands where cruising people have had to physically leave an anchorage because the natives, curious about them and the boat, would come and stay. Yet, the encounter was not a bitter one. The decision to leave would be more of a, "Wow, we love you, but we just need some privacy." It's a different kind of disruption in some parts of the Caribbean and Mediter-

ranean. Resentful of the "rich" on their yachts, the locals can be tragically hostile in the port areas where tourists have fouled the air. "In St. Vincent, things have gone to hell," a cruising sailor wrote me recently. "In Kingston, I couldn't go on shore at night. And forget about Colombia."

3. A fabled Pacific port. Nice people, beautiful island, good food supplies. Only sour note was: "The guy at immigration. We gave him our visas when we arrived. No problem. Suddenly when we're ready to depart, there's a problem. It will cost twenty-five dollars to fix the problem. I say to hell with the problem. We haven't had one since we left Florida. So we go out quietly the next morning and forget about it, but I wonder how many people forked up the twenty-five dollars before us."

What do you do about the official corruption? Not much, except avoid the worst spots (the west coast of Africa is a perennial headache). Says a fellow who's cruised his 35-foot yawl a good bit overseas: "Being a timid sort, I comply fully with instructions of consuls in the U.S. and have had no problems. I have heard people loudly complaining of, say, Ecuadorian bureaucracy. I regarded them as people who cut corners and expected to bluff their way through. Use the land analogy. I have had considerable difficulty when crossing from Kenya to Tanganyika by routes not specified as normal transit routes by the governments involved."

Another fellow, now based with his ketch in California, has this advice: "During my cruising days, technicalities were minimal. I was detained for nine days in Mexico for having carelessly disclosed that we had stopped for a night in a Costa Rican port where there were no customs or immigration authorities, hence, no proper clearance. The cure would have been lots of cash directly to the Mexican authorities, but they finally tired of waiting. It's best to know what kind of legal and political climate is in a port just before arriving. You can get this by word of mouth, recent magazine articles, or journals like the *Flying Fish* [see p. 158]. Some places really should be avoided if you have notice that they're laying for you. By the same token, some ports may have cleaned up their acts recently and cruisers might tend to avoid them because of older impressions."

4. It was a variation of "no room at the inn." It happened to one man in Durban, South Africa, when he and some other cruising people were told their stay in port might be limited to two months or less because of congestion on the international jetty. At that time, the jetty was packed, with 15 more boats expected that season.

"The yacht clubs in Hong Kong, Singapore, Manila, and Cape Town used to entertain and help you out with enthusiasm," writes this cruising veteran in Durban. "Now they say, 'No more room.' They'll send you to a fishing pier or so-and-so bay or anchorage." No use fulminating about the way things used to be. With more and more people cruising, there are apt to be changes. Be positive and think that it's still much better than living in suburbia and commuting to New York.

5. It happened in Argentina. The boat needed work badly as she limped into port after a rough passage, but there were few imported supplies and the local gear was for weekend sailors. Stainless steel? Naval bronze? The locals didn't have much use for it, though they were terrifically *simpatico* and troubled by the yacht's dilemma. The solution was an expensive wire back to a U.S. supplier, followed by an expensive airlift of supplies. Fortunately, the replacement parts arrived within a couple of weeks. Friends of this boat owner had had to wait six weeks on a Pacific island for much-needed engine parts.

Much the same situation faced the American sloop in the Azores when the owner decided to head for Portugal rather than England as originally intended. The problem in this case was that no one had remembered or thought to bring Portuguese charts and there was no time to order them. So two crewmembers laboriously copied the charts of another American vessel that was in port at the same time. Five hours of tracing in the cabin and they had it. Moral: Always plan for the worst. Carry extra parts and any charts you might conceivably need.

6. Some Central American ports are ferocious to foreigners.

One yacht's owner and his wife decided it would be OK to lock up and take a walk through town. They got back in an hour and found the boat cleaned out—binoculars, camera, sextant, all the booze. They learned the hard way that you hire a guard for a boat if you leave it.

If possible, keep someone from the crew on board all the time. Or tie up next to another foreign yacht and split watches. Watch the dinghy. In some ports, you can wake up at three in the morning and find someone trying to rip it off. One couple would have lost theirs if the ropes hadn't been backed up by a wire locked firmly to a genoa car (the hardware that carries the genoa sail on the sail tracks).

7. Three customs officials, all dressed like four-star generals, came on board and the boat's owner was nervous. So many questions; such belligerence. He was sure they were going to find something wrong. So he made the mistake of offering the chief a bottle of Scotch and suddenly three pairs of eyes glinted: "Those are good binoculars . . . you know there seems to be a little irregularity here I didn't notice before . . ." It's OK to offer a glass of wine, at most, but don't offer anything to officials that murmurs "bribe" or they'll figure you're an easy mark. Another precaution: Keep everything that "glitters" out of sight while they're aboard. Out of sight, out of mind.

8. At New Zealand a yacht owner with a dog on board was told, politely, that he'd have to post a bond that the animal wouldn't leave the boat. Every few days, inspectors from the agricultural department would wander by to make sure he was indeed staying on board. In other countries, animals can be subject to quarantine, or even mercy killing. The rules seem stringent on the surface, because voyagers traditionally have liked the companionship of cats or dogs on their boats. They've come about because owners have not always kept their pets on board, or kept rabies and other shots current. There have even been cases—as in Australia—where animals have escaped from ships and have multiplied to menacing proportions in their new environment.

Certainly, a lot of boats carry animals. But if you're planning a long voyage, it might be the wisest thing to find homes for your pets before you leave rather than restrict the ports you can enter or incur fines or quarantine expenses.

9. Virtuously, they renewed the stainless-steel rigging every four years on their sloop. "But not the tangs attaching the wire at the masthead. That's a mistake," admits her owner. "A thousand miles east of Barbados, a tang parted and we lost both upper shrouds and had to continue under storm trysail alone, using the spinnaker halyard and topping lift boomed out athwartships with two spinnaker poles which were vanged and led to the number five winches. I think this saved the mast." (To put this in plain words; the top-of-the-mast attachment, which holds the support wires for the mast at its sides, broke. Since both wires were collapsed, the boat had to continue under a small storm trysail alone. A jury rig was accomplished, using two sail positioning ropes held by two poles and attached to winches at the sides.)

Conditions were clear; the crew was experienced; the owner was clearheaded. It doesn't always happen that way. A sudden emergency, whether it's the loss of a fitting, a bad injury, or a run-in by a freighter, can be met in either of two ways. If the crew is disciplined and experienced, the reactions are appropriate. If the crew is inexperienced and badly frightened, they can be shocked into psychological immobility or useless reactions.

Consider what might happen if a crewmember falls overboard. You could find his companions engaging in all kinds of useless reactions: shocked staring into space, crying, or pointless activity like lowering the sails or trying to swim to the man's aid. There's a sense of unreality about a catastrophe—you think that it really can't be happening, or that it can't be happening to you. When the *Andrea Doria* was sinking 200 miles off Nantucket, some people in a boat coming to the rescue actually thought that the searchlights picking out people in the water were all part of a water carnival! Incredible? Yes. But until you've been involved in a sudden crisis, you can't appreciate the strange workings of the human mind.

What causes an emergency? The same thing, often though,

that causes a safe voyage: the human element. Neglect and ignorance probably cause more accidents than you'd care to think about.

We can look at an emergency situation as having three levels of cure. Two are preventive and one is a solution to the trouble.

The first level is the truest prevention: a carefully tended and equipped boat on which nothing is left to chance. If you go back to the story we started with, you'll see that if the tangs had been replaced along with the rigging, there wouldn't have been any danger of losing the mast and no interruption in the voyage. Look around your boat and you can come up with dozens of possible emergencies. Bad electrical connections, for instance. Replacing them can prevent a spark that could cause problems calling for solution by fire extinguisher, a distress signal, even a life raft.

At the second level are kinds of equipment whose purpose is primarily preventive and highly specialized. Among them you can tick off:

a. a gas sniffer for the engine compartment, an erratic monster to maintain, but a useful one (in a pinch, a good stand-in preventive is the human nose, but we seldom remember to use it);

b. an extractor fan, certainly a blower for a gas engine;

c. radar reflector or an electronic device that picks up radar signals and flashes a warning. (One possibility is the Marine Check Radar Detector, imported by International Marine Instruments, Joshua Slocum Dock, Stamford, Connecticut 06902. It's a hefty investment at about $130, but it will sound a comforting alarm if it detects a ship's radar signal, which means that you can grab some more sleep instead of anxiously scanning the horizon.);

d. safety harness for working on deck, about as popular as seat belts and probably more useful;

e. fog horn.

These examples are common sense, but the list could go on. Radar (if you can afford it), good navigation, even proper seamanship, can all be considered preventive under certain circumstances.

The third level of coping is equipment that resolves the problem: The choice of the right safety equipment can mean a speedy solution on one hand, and avoidance of frustration and disaster on the other. Dangerously inadequate for local sailing, let alone an ocean voyage, are a few time-expired distress signals, some old life jackets, and a dinghy. Naturally, all equipment has to be in good working order. The bare minimum for a boat that doesn't venture out to sea would be:

at least half a dozen distress signals
a fire extinguisher in good order
dinghy
built-in bilge pump, plus a hand pump
safety harness
boarding ladder (imperative for man-overboard situations)
a couple of life buoys
life jackets for the entire crew and passengers
heaving line

For coastal cruising and short sea passages, you would want to add:

an EPIRB (emergency position-indicating radio beacon)
radar reflector
life-buoy light
fire blanket
inflatable life raft (a good make such as Avon is dependable and
    worth the extra cost)

Any boat making extended ocean passages should invariably carry equipment and parts needed to effect jury rigs or temporary repairs. Under the section on tools, we mentioned that an ocean voyager should literally be able to build a boat with the equipment on board. Certainly, he should have a collision mat (either a commercial variety or a strong homemade one), a well-stocked life raft (including emergency food and water), and basic materials like wooden plugs, wire cutters, extra stainless-steel rigging, and pieces of tubing. In addition, a water dye-marker pack is a good idea as it tremendously aids in air searches.

Here are a few random pieces of advice: Carry *valid* passports for *all* crew and visas if required by the country. Don't carelessly allow your passports to lapse on a long voyage; you can be detained for weeks, even months, getting your credentials straightened out.

Have plenty of crew lists—some countries require up to five copies.

Carry a big ship's seal. The more ornate, the better.

Keep some spare bits of colored cloth on hand so you can whip up foreign courtesy flags.

Pay customs only the charges specified in print on forms, and demand receipts for everything. If you're asked for more money than specified, act confused and a little dense. They may get tired of fooling around and charge you the correct rate.

Finally, be philosophical. As one seasoned cruiser says: "Paper work is a little problem, especially if you treat it as a fun experience—you can learn a lot from customs officials."

I feel a little guilty retelling some of these stories; they are all so negative. Friends will warn of hazards—greedy customs men and all the rest—but most cruising people when they look back on their voyages remember things like a rollicking night at a harbor pub, the easy roll of the yacht at sea, the nights at anchor under starry skies, a hot cup of coffee on the afterdeck in the morning, a moonlit drift over a phosphorescent sea.

Hang the dangers (but not the customs man, much as you'd like to). The really important thing is to go.

APPENDIX A
A LIBRARY FOR THE BOAT
BUYER OR BUILDER

If you have trouble locating any of these books locally, there's one place that has them all—and just about any other boating title you can think of: International Marine Publishing, 21 Elm Street, Camden, Maine 04843. Write them for a copy of their catalog with current prices and ordering information—or you can get a copy bound into most issues of *National Fisherman*.

Voyaging Under Power, by Capt. Robert P. Beebe. An almost forgotten area, the long-distance power yacht, covered by the foremost authority, a cruising man and designer both.

Understanding Boat Design, by Edward S. Brewer and Jim Betts. Sort of a beginner's text, it manages to unravel some basic questions, like the cost of plans and the business relationship between designer and owner.

Boatbuilding, by Howard I. Chapelle. Another bible. The section on lofting alone is worth the price, which was a hefty $17.50 at this writing.

Trimarans: An Introduction, by D. H. Clarke. Now a standard work on multi-hulls, Clarke even gets into explaining chartering and berthing.

Coastwise and Offshore Cruising Wrinkles, by Thomas E. Colvin.

A designer and cruising man of long experience, Colvin's ideas are always thought-provoking, especially his espousal of the junk rig.

Skene's Elements of Yacht Design, revised by Francis S. Kinney. Starting with basics, this is the bible of naval architecture, with a lot of information you can't find anywhere else.

The Mariner's Catalog, vols. 1–4 (and may there be many more). These have such a wealth of information on good books, boats, tools, and all kinds of odds and ends, you'll wonder how you got along without them.

From a Bare Hull, by Ferenc Mate. This is a step-by-step look at how one homebuilder finished a bare hull, in this case a Westsail 32, though the information applies equally well to any cruising design.

Customizing Your Boat, by Ian Nicolson. A practical book with detailed drawings and instructions on all sorts of modifications, from the structural to those that make everyday life a little easier.

Ocean Voyaging, by David M. Parker. A pragmatic, sometimes impertinent, often funny look at what constitutes a good long-range cruiser. Parker writes with 100,000 miles of blue-water sailing to his credit.

The Long Distance Cruiser, by Bill Rothrock. More irreverent personal opinions. The author is pretty outspoken about designers, builders, and, yes, owners.

The Ocean Sailing Yacht, by Donald M. Street, Jr. Well on its way to being a classic, this book manages to cover the whole complex machine that is the modern cruising boat. Street writes like a knowledgeable friend, no pompousness.

Boat Repairs and Conversions, by Michael Verney. If you're interested in getting afloat on a budget, here's your guide. It goes from finding a hull that's fixable—whether wood or fiber glass—to installing a heating system and interior joiner work.

Boatbuilding and Repairing with Fiberglass, by Melvin D. C. Willis. Since fiber glass is the way we're all going, this book may keep you out of trouble. The section on repairs is nothing less than a public service to the impecunious owner.

APPENDIX B
WHERE TO GET A BARE HULL OR
KIT BOAT

Hull prices listed below are FOB the factory and subject to change. The information in the second column is in the following order:

Length overall/beam/draft
Displacement of completed boat
Sail area
Price of completed boat

Blue Buoy Yacht Co., 1922 Oak Street, Torrance, California 90501
This company specializes in kit boats, and the 31 and 45 have been completed by several people as liveaboards. The 24 and 26 are rarely sold as kits as the difference in cost is so little. Paul Blue tells us, "It's usually advisable to allow us to install some of the bulkheads and floors to help hold the shape of the hull. At any rate, we advise and guide the purchaser so he is not left out in the cold after he acquires his boat." When we spoke to him, two fellows were completing their hulls in the Blue Buoy yard.

Del Rey 24	24′/7′ 10″/3′ 8″ 4,500 lbs. 272 sq. ft. $6,500	$4,695	The Blue Buoy prices we quote are all for hull, deck, ballast, and rudder installed.

Del Rey 26	26'/8'/4' 5,800 lbs. 271 sq. ft. $7,950	$4,995	Formerly the Meridian Seaquest; Blue Buoy purchased the tooling. This is a clipper-bowed, spade rudder, fin keel design.
Del Rey 31	31'/10' 2"/5' 10,000 lbs. 428 sq. ft. $24,500	$9,500	Designed for cruising and liveaboard, has a spade rudder and fairly long keel. Additional components available (main bulkhead and mast support, $325, etc.).
Del Rey 45	45'/12' 6"/6' 6" 33,000 lbs. 997 sq. ft. $75,000 and up	$20,000	Rudder installation includes pedestal steering. Some sample prices for other components: chain plates, $700; tanks, $4 per gallon; 1" plywood bulkheads, $400 each.

Blue Water Boats, Box 625, Woodinville, Washington 98072

As the name says, this company builds a boat designed for ocean passages. The Ingrid 38, as she's called, is a William Atkin adaptation of Colin Archer's well-known double-ender. The fellow who runs Blue Water, Jerry Husted, has this to say: "Usually long hours of conversation take place prior to any sale. We try to define the character of the boat-to-be and give examples of the spending decisions that have to be made. The owner begins with the plans and either decides on his own layout or spends several hundred dollars with a good naval architect, which we believe is the best expenditure he can make after buying a boat from us." Husted will invite an owner to spend a day glassing his bulkheads in the shop so he understands the right way to work with fiber glass. He also helps with purchasing (extending his own builder's discount) and has study plans and a sketchbook of interiors (done by Jay Benford) available.

| *Ingrid 38* | 37′ 8″/11′ 4″/5′ 8″
26,000 lbs.
887 sq. ft.
up to $60,000 | $8,875 | Bare hull. Deck and cabin top temporarily through-bolted to hull is an additional $7,000. A price list on other components is available. |
| | | $34,415 | A basic kit that includes hull, deck, bulkheads, ballast, plywood interior, rudder, engine, tanks, and wood spars. |

Cape Cod Shipbuilding Co., Wareham, Massachusetts 02571
Cape Cod has sold about a half dozen bare hulls of the Blue Chip, mostly to local people who can visit the yard and get their questions answered. Ernest Goodwin, who heads the firm, has this philosophy about bare-hull boatbuilders: "If a man buys the hull thinking he's going to save a lot of money and wants the boat in the water within a year, then I'd say he's licked before he begins. But if he is a skilled wood-worker and can spend two years working on it, then he'll do a professional job."

| *Blue Chip* | 29′ 10″/9′ 6″/4′ 3″
7,500 lbs.
465 sq. ft.
$25,900 | $14,500 | Capt. Nat himself designed the Blue Chip hull with her overhangs, bowsprit, and graceful wineglass sections, while his oldest son, Sidney DeW. Herreshoff, designed the modern rig. |

Chinook Yachts, Ste. 1-3260 Edgemont Boulevard, North Vancouver, British Columbia, Canada
The 37 is a motor sailer design from Stan Huntingford. Hull No. 2, which came out of the molds in January, was ordered as a kit. Chinook will supply detailed rigging and interior plans as well as wiring diagrams and so on.

| *Chinook 37* | 37'/11' 8"/5' 18,600 lbs. $65,000 | $16,000 | Hull and deck bonded, parts for rudder, pilot house, swim grid, hatches, and transom door. |
| | | $25,000 | Hull and deck with pilot house, swim grid, floors, tanks, keel, rudder, and bulkheads installed. |

Clark Craft Boat Co., 16 Aqua Lane, Tonawanda, New York 14150
For almost 30 years, Clark Craft has been supplying homebuilders with plans, frames, hull kits, and backup material where needed. Their separate powerboat and sailboat catalogs list a total of over 300 designs from seven to 77 feet, in fiber glass, plywood, ferrocement, and steel. Probably the best way to get acquainted with their boats is to order a set of their catalogs (complete with their *Boat Builder's Guide*) for $2. Among others, they offer designs by New Zealand's Richard Hartley as well as Bruce Roberts. Designs run the gamut from houseboats to ocean cruisers. One example:

| *Spray (Bruce Roberts version)* | 37' 6"/14' 4"/4' 2" 32,000 lbs. 833 sq. ft. | $5,000 (approx.) | Clark Craft supplies material kits for building the hull, deck, and cabin structure of many of its larger boat designs. The $5,000 figure here varies, depending, for example, on whether you wanted to build |

this particular boat in
fiber glass, or C-Flex.
Roberts adapted
plans for Slocum's
Spray in this design
and drew up five dif-
ferent deck plans and
interiors. Study
plans that include the
five versions sell for
$15.

Dreadnought Boatworks, Box 221, Carpinteria, California 93013
If you fancy John Hanna's Tahiti ketch, Dreadnought Boatworks has
the fiber glass version, similar to *Adios*, which won the 1964 Blue-
water Cruising Medal and made two circumnavigations. One of
these fiber-glass Dreadnoughts sailed from San Francisco to Honolulu in 21 days.

Dread-	32'/10'/4' 9"	$7,500	Bare hull only. Deck
nought	19,980 lbs.		and cabin is an addi-
32	550 sq. ft.		tional $3,425 in-
	$45,000		stalled.
		$28,250	Sailaway Kit, with
			sails and engine.
			You finish the inte-
			rior.
		$29,750	The Campout
			Cutter, as they call
			it. There's a rough
			interior with basic
			necessities.

Durbeck's, Inc., 4504 28th Street, West Bradenton, Florida 33505

D38 Cutter	41'/11' 4"/5'	$8,850	Hull Only.
or Ketch	19,200 lbs.	$40,106	Water Kit.
	$65,000 (cutter)		

D46 Ketch	46' 9"/13' 8"/	$13,319	Hull only.
	4' 11"	$68,232	Water Kit. A boat
	35,000 lbs.		capable of motoring
	1,270 sq. ft.		on her own bottom to
	$119,500		a location where you
			can finish her your-
			self.

Dyer, 57 Miller Street, Warren, Rhode Island 02885

R. G. Lundstrom, manager of Dyer, says, "While we haven't offered kit boats with detailed finishing plans, and don't want the kind of business where the amateur phones, 'I cut the bulkheads two inches too short—what can I do?', we have found that many a man who has proven himself able to work creditably with carpenter tools can save a considerable amount of money and have the pleasure of completing his own boat. Experience on smaller and simpler hulls is almost a prerequisite. Otherwise, you may be biting off more than you can chew." Lundstrom asked two men who were finishing Dyer 29s if they had kept track of their time—each had exceeded 1,000 hours. "Since one was a professional pattern maker and the other an electrical-power-plant installer, it would probably take the average person longer."

Dyer 29	28' 6"/9' 5"/2' 6"	$4,200	The bare hull, one
	6,700 lbs.		designed by Nick
	$23,400		Potter and based on
			the lines of com-
			mercial Down East
			fishing boats. Dyer
			has a price list on
			other components,
			from cockpit coaming
			to deck hardware.
Dyer 40	39' 8"/12' 5"	$8,800	Also designed by
	15,000 lbs.		Nick Potter, this is a
	$80,000 and up		larger version of the
			29-footer.

Ferro-Boat Builders, Inc., 2 Binnacle Lane, Mt. Harmony, Maryland 20836
This company has been in operation more than five years and has built a number of ferrocement hulls, primarily liveaboard and ocean cruising types, to designs by Tom Colvin, Al Mason, Bruce Ningham, and the like. Jake Bauer, the president, says, "Our business is primarily building custom hulls and I keep an active design file. A customer comes in with his set of requirements and we come up with five or six designs that fill them. We're relatively small builders, so we can personally follow up the progress of the kit builders. We answer the phones ourselves—you don't get a secretary." Bauer helps with some of the difficult jobs, like installing the engine, rigging, or laying teak decks, if the owner wants it. As an example of his prices, Peter Ibold's Endurance 40 bare hull with decks and ballast is $14,800.

Gannon Yachts, Box 1058, Petaluma, California 94952
The Freya 39 is a fiber-glass version of the Halvorsen Freya, with the shear line raised several inches for more interior space. The original Freya won the Sydney–Hobart three years in succession. On one cruise, she covered 8,000 miles from Australia to San Francisco via the Hawaiian Islands in 59 sailing days.

Freya 39	39′ 3″/11′ 3″/6′ 23,000 lbs. $61,000	$36,250	Sailaway Kit, including hull with ballast, cabin sole, six bulkheads, rudder, pedestal steering, spars, and rigging.
		$8,750	Bare hull only. Deck is an additional $5,500.

Glander Boats, Inc., RR. No. 1, Box 1107, Tavernier, Florida 33070

Cay Sloop	27′ 6″/8′/3′ 6,800 lbs. 350 sq. ft.	$2,182	Bare hull and plans for finishing. Other components are available, for example, the deck assembly is $1,937.62, and the

			hatches installed are about $231. Glander does not sell finished boats, incidentally, only kit boats.
Tavana	33'/10'/3' 12,000 lbs. 553 sq. ft. (yawl rig)	$4,145	Bare hull with plans for finishing. Deck assembly is $3,709, rudder, $388, etc. As with the Cay Sloop, Glander will help the homebuilder buy an engine, masts, sails, hardware, and so on at a savings.

Hidden Harbor Boat Works, Inc., 2029 Whitfield Park Avenue, Sarasota, Florida 33580
Hidden Harbor will finish this design to any stage of completion and Stephen Seaton, the president, says they can build subcomponent or prefab units for the owner to install himself.

56' Motor Yacht	56' 7"	Price on request	This buys the hull (Airex core) with four bulkheads in place. Several profiles are possible for the standard hull.

Kells Corp., 1 Shove Street, Tiverton, Rhode Island 02878

Kells 28 Outrider	27' 7"/9' 2"/4' 7" 6,800 lbs. 375 sq. ft. $16,900	$7,700	This includes hull and deck with rubrail, major bulkheads, six opening ports, hatches, rudder, mast, boom, and stainless-steel rigging. Shipping cradle, $210.

Luger Industries, Inc., 3800 West Highway 13, Burnsville, Minnesota 55337

Rennold and Ormond Luger started their company 24 years ago when they rented a deserted supermarket and started putting together a kit for a 12-foot plywood runabout. Now they sell 500 fiber glass boat kits a year. After nearly a quarter of a century, they're very professional. Gerald Lannery of Illinois, who completed their 22-foot Caribbean design, puts it this way: "Each wood part was stamped with a number, and I just followed the blueprints which showed the location of each numbered part and the detailed instructions. The instructions were numbered step by step." The Lugers sell accessory kits with everything you need to complete and outfit each of their boats, except for a few specialized items like winches and sail track. And they have a toll-free "hotline" at the plant so they can answer any questions about completing their boats. A few finished boats are always on hand in Burnsville if you want to see what you'll end up with, and the Lugers will be happy to discuss financing if you need some help.

Trade-winds Sloop	26′ 5″/7′ 11″/2′ 2″ 2,600 lbs. 235 sq. ft.	$2,995	This is the Hull Kit, which buys the one-piece hull, deck, hatch covers, bolts, bonding materials, and standing rigging.
		$3,529	The Complete Kit, including all the above plus precut cabin interior parts, rudder, and deck hardware.
Monte Carlo Cruiser	24′ 8″/8′/1′ 2,300 lbs.	$2,495	Hull Kit, .ncluding hull sections, deck and cabin sections, hatches, fasteners, and bonding materials.

Marine Technical Services, 2218 Marine View Dr. Tacoma, Washington 98422

The 34 is a modernized version of a double-ender built in 1949, to a design by Stan Huntingford. She is long-keeled with a bowsprit and boomkin and is slack-bilged. Patterns, bulkheads, plans, and a kit builder's manual are available.

True North	34' 2"/11'/5' 6"	$13,000	Hull and deck. Other components available include rudder ($600), bulkheads installed ($1,000), etc.
34	22,506 lbs.		
	$48,000		
		$24,500	The wet kit, with the hull, deck, bulkheads, ballast, tanks, cabin sole, Volve engine rudder, ports, hatches, and mast step.

Matlack Yacht Builders, Inc., West Salerno Road, Route 3, Stuart, Florida 33494

Stuart Angler	33' 2"/11'/2' 10"	$6,850	Bare hull of this Ned Mairs-designed fishing boat, modeled on the lines of Down East lobstermen. She can be adapted as an open fisherman, sportfisherman with flying bridge, cruiser, or skin-diving boat.
	8,660 lbs.		
	(price on request)		

McCutcheon Boat Works, Ferry Avenue, Charlevoix, Michigan 49720

30' Ketch	30'/9' 6"/4' 9"	$4,000	Hull only. This is a cruising ketch. When we spoke to McCutcheon in the
	11,800 lbs.		
	470 sq. ft.		
	(price on request)		

summer, 12 had been built and, of these, 10 had been completed by their owners. Hull and deck would be about $7,000.

Thomas D. C. Morris, Yacht Builder, Southwest Harbor, Maine 04679

Designer C. W. Paine built the first Frances 26 for his own use, and Morris took his molds from her. She is a sturdy double-ender and, as Paine comments, "Load Frances with your world cruising gear and she won't show it." Paine's drawings and notes on construction and material are available for $250.

Frances 26	26'/8'/3' 10" 6,800 lbs. 337 sq. ft. $19,000	$3,600	Bare hull. A list of prices for further work is available: ballast (3,400 lbs. lead), $2,100; deck installed, $3,300, etc.
Leigh 30	30'/9' 7"/4' 7" 9,010 lbs. 440 sq. ft. $35,000	$4,300	Bare hull.

New England Boatbuilders, Inc., Harbor Road North, Mattapoisett, Massachusetts 02739

New England offers a hull designed by Jerry Cartwright, as well as two other distinctive vessels. John Feroce, president of the company, says they offer full consultation to kit builders. He advises having critical points like the welding of the stainless-steel rudder post on the Nantucket 40, shaft alignment, installation of the stuffing box, and so on, done by the yard.

Nantucket 40	40'/11' 3"/5' 10" 23,500 lbs. 829 sq. ft. $90,000	$14,500	This buys the bare hull with Airex core construction ($13,000 without an Airex core). Some other figures on the blue-

			water cruiser: 10,000 lbs. lead ballast, $4,400; five bulkheads, $1,495; deck in place, $3,850; doghouse/cockpit tub in place, $2,600; rudder hung and fitted, $1,500.
Meadow-lark	37′/8′/18″ min. 10,000 lbs. 456 sq. ft. $35,800	$4,200	Bare hull only on this classic Herreshoff-designed ketch. Other figures: deck, $3,800; ballast, $2,000; rough interior, $2,800.
Margaret D	24′ 7″/8′/3′ 4″ 5,250 lbs. 346 sq. ft. $12,500 (ketch) $11,500 (sloop)	$2,100	Bare hull. Ketch or sloop versions of this sturdy little cruiser are available. The deck is $1,850.

Jarvis Newman, Yacht Builder, Southwest Harbor, Maine 04679
"Our main business is building hulls," says Newman, "however, we do complete one now and then."

Pemaquid	25′/8′ 8″/4′ 7,000 lbs. 432 sq. ft.	$4,900	Bare hull of this fiber glass Friendship Sloop.
Dictator	31′/11′/5′ 17,500 lbs. 761 sq. ft.	$7,300	Bare hull of this 31-foot classic Friendship Sloop in fiber glass.
Newman Lobster-boat	32′/11′/3′ 6″ 14,000 lbs.	$7,100	Bare hull. A traditional Maine lobster-boat hull designed by Ralph Stanley, suitable for pleasure or commercial use.

Newman	36'/11'/3' 6"	$7,900	Bare Hull. A Maine
Lobster-	17,000 lbs.		lobsterboat hull de-
boat			signed by Raymond
			Bunker.

Nor'Sea Yachts, 2919 Gardena Avenue, Long Beach, California 90806
The Nor'Sea 27, designed by Lyle Hess on the lines of double-ended North Sea workboats, is not only a blue-water cruising boat, but legally transportable. The boat is available in several states of completion. Dean Wixom at Nor'Sea can answer any questions.

Nor'Sea 27	27'/8'/3' 6"	$4,250	Hull only. Deck is an
	7,000 lbs.		additional $1,950.
	376 sq. ft.	$8,950	This buys the hull,
	$28,800		deck, rudder, hatches,
			ballast, and tempo-
			rary cabin sole.
		$14,500	The Sailaway Kit,
			with unfinished in-
			terior, but all rigging
			and spars. Engine in-
			stalled is an addi-
			tional $2,950.

North Star Yachts, Ltd., Huron Industrial Park, Huron Park, Ontario, Canada NOM 1YO

North	26'/9'/4'	$6,499	This basic kit consists
Star 26	4,598 lbs.		of the hull and deck
	281 sq. ft.		with 2,000 pounds of
	$10,995		lead ballast, one
			structural bulkhead,
			rudder and shaft,
			hatch covers, and
			headliner. The
			builder supplies a
			manual of all the
			component kits
			needed to complete
			the boat.

North Star 30	29′ 11″/9′ 6″/5′ 3″ 8,000 lbs. 399 sq. ft. $22,575	$9,899	Same as above.

Northern Boatbuilding, TransCanada Highway, Cobble Hill, British Columbia, Canada

Ernie Norris of Northern Boatbuilding points out that the hulls are built to exceed Lloyd's standards and have an Airex foam core. The kit prices on the following include hull and deck with bulkheads installed and hatches supplied loose. Rudder, ballast, engine, and other components are available.

Pacific 30	30′ $25,900	$8,650	A fast cruiser with racing potential.
Roberts 32	32′/10′/5′ 6″ $29,680	$9,900	A moderate-displacement offshore cruising boat with a long keel and large skeg protecting the rudder.
Roberts 36	36′ 9″/11′/4′ $35,976	$12,800	A traditional long-keel cruising boat.
Roberts 36 Motor sailer	36′ 9″/11′/4′ $39,900	$NA	A fast, oceangoing motor sailer with full keel.
Roberts 38	38′ $39,900	$14,200	Another fast passage-maker with a full keel.
Roberts 44	44′ 8″/12′ 9″/6′ $48,500	$17,000	Large cruising vessel, suitable for a family or couple.

Portsmouth Yacht Co., Box 285, Portsmouth, Rhode Island 02871

Eastward Ho	23′ 8″/8′ 8″/3′ 10″ 7,000 lbs. 283 sq. ft. $16,550	$3,868	Hull, deck, and rudder of this Eldredge-McInnis design.

Rawson, Inc., 15014 N.E. 90th Street, Redmond, Washington 98052
Rawson builds a 30-foot sailboat hull based on a 1959 design by
William Garden. They also have 32-, 38-, and 42-foot semidisplace-
ment powerboat hulls, designed by Edwin Monk.

Rawson 30	30′ 6″/9′/5′ 12,000 lbs. 410 sq. ft. $32,000	$11,500	This buys the hull and deck, ballast, bulkheads, cabin sole, and chain plates. Plus whatever advice you need from Rawson.

Reliance Sailing Craft Co., Box 693, St. Laurent, Montreal, P.Q.,
Canada

Reliance 44	44′ 4″/11′ 8″/6′ 2″ 28,000 lbs. 905 sq. ft.	on request	This is Pierre Meunier's design for offshore cruising, available in kit form only with the hull and deck joined, deck-house, bulkheads (tacked in or permanently glassed in to the hull and under-deck), chain plates, attachment brackets, and rudder assembly (loose or installed). One-inch balsa core is used in the hull, deck, and deckhouse. Ketch or cutter rig.

Rosborough Boats, Ltd., Box 188, Armdale, Nova Scotia, Canada.
B3L 459
James D. Rosborough builds traditional wood ketches, schooners,
brigantines, and barques, from 30 to 100 feet. As he says, "We offer
vessels in any stage of completion, from a keel lying on the ground
to a complete sailaway vessel. We have, in the past, built some bare

hulls for owners who finished them. One did a very creditable job and sailed the vessel from Nova Scotia via the Caribbean to Vancouver, British Columbia, where he entered her in the charter trade. We offer to build the hulls, supply building plans, obtain materials at discount, and provide a reasonable amount of architects' consultations. This total service package on a hull is $300 to $700. With the recession being what it is, this part of our operation is gaining an increasing popularity." Designs available range from the R-30 (30') to the Discovery (85'). We've listed only a representative, and very popular, design below. A complete catalog of plans is $3.

Privateer	45' 10"/13' 3"/ 5' 11" 42,880 lbs. sail plan varies about $64,000	$23,000	Bare hull with deck, outside ballast, keel, rudder, with caulking and painting done. The Privateer is Rosborough's most popular design to date, with 45 hulls launched. It's available as a ketch, schooner, or brigantine and is heavily built of Northeastern pine (mahogany at extra cost) on oak. Decks are plywood, fiber-glassed.

C. E. Ryder Corp., Box 274, 47 Gooding Avenue, Bristol, Rhode Island 02809

Ryder offers this Thomas Gillmer-designed double-ender, in several stages of completion, from bare hull to finished vessel.

Gillmer 31	31'/9' 6"/4' 7" 13,600 lbs. 447 sq. ft. $39,500	$5,450 $19,690	Hull only. Sailaway kit. Includes sails and rigging, but not engine. Interior is unfinished.

Safari Marine, 776 W. 16th Street, Costa Mesa, California 92627
When we talked to the builder, he was just about ready to start production on this very traditional-looking cutter. Actually, Safari is not a new company, having built sedan cruisers for the past ten years, though owner Yale Wittmer professes he is a "ragman" at heart.

Safari 36	36' 8"/11'/5' 9" 17,800 lbs. 1,018 sq. ft.	$12,900	This buys the hull, deck, and rudder, with plans showing various cabin layouts.

Soverel Marine, Inc., 2225 Idlewilde Road, North Palm Beach, Florida 33403
Conrad Heinold, a home builder in Wilmington, Delaware, completed a Soverel 28 (no longer available) and told us he got all the help he needed: "Bill Soverel was very helpful throughout the entire project and arranged the purchase of anything we requested." Heinold was able to give us some time/cost figures, pointing out that his experience consisted of building an 18-foot Seagull sloop a few years earlier. He started out with the hull and deck bonded together and with the rudder installed, finishing the boat in about 1,000 hours of weekend and evening work over a period of a year. Total cost was about $10,500 (with outboard engine).

Soverel 26	26'/10'/4' 9" 5,000 lbs. 350 sq. ft. $14,900	$9,900	All prices are for the hull with deck, headliner, cabin sole, bulkheads, berths, and galley molding. All outfitting items can be purchased through Soverel at cost plus ten percent.
Soverel 37	36' 6"/9' 4"/3' 6" 12,000 lbs. 550 sq. ft. $32,900	$12,500	See above.

Soverel 41	41′ 3″/11′/4′ 5″ 18,000 lbs. 750 sq. ft. $49,900	$18,500	See above.
Soverel 48	48′/13′/4′ 6″ 28,000 lbs. 858 sq. ft. $125,000	$29,000	See above.

Spencer Boats, Ltd., 1240 Twigg Road, Richmond, British Columbia, Canada V6V 1M5

Les McBurney at Spencer tells us: "Since our models range from 31 to 51 feet, we feel that most of our customers are relatively knowledgeable sailors who are generally aware of the extent of the undertaking in completion of the boat. We try to caution them that an extensive boatbuilding project should only be undertaken as a form of recreation and that any savings achieved will depend on their ability as a contractor, finisher, etc. We don't attempt to provide a completely precut, preassembled finishing kit because this adds substantially to the cost of finishing and limits the ability to adapt the layout. We do, however, make the shop and its personnel available for consultation. Our designers, John Brandlemayr Ltd., are available for advice on changing rig, structure, and so on."

Spencer 31	31′/9′ 2″/5′ 9,000 lbs. 410 sq. ft. $32,135	$5,395	Hull only. All Spencer prices are FOB Sidney or Richmond, B.C.
		$11,975	Hull with deck attached, fuel and water tanks, bulkheads and cabin sole installed. No ballast.
		$20,775	Headliner, unfinished interior joinerwork, rough electrical work.
Spencer 35	35′/9′ 6″/5′ 3″ 12,000 lbs. 487 sq. ft. $46,125	$7,350	Hull only. This is a traditional family cruising boat with a long keel.

		$17,225	Hull with deck, cabin sole, main bulkheads, ballast.
		$30,685	All the above, plus rough electrical work, unfinished joiner-work, and headliner. Interior needs painting and installations.
Spencer 42	42′ 3″/11′ 4″/6′ 19,000 lbs. 778 sq. ft. (ketch rig) $75,285	$11,580	Hull only. The 42 is a traditional-looking, medium-displacement cruiser with full keel.
		$25,565	Hull with deck attached, main bulkheads, cabin sole, ballast.
		$30,685	The above, plus rough electrical work, unfinished joiner-work, and headliner.
Spencer 44	43′ 9″/11′ 6″/ 6′ 6″ 24,000 lbs. 846 sq. ft. (ketch rig) $82,855	$12,765	Hull only. The 44 is a center cockpit yacht, with full keel.
		$29,295	Hull with deck, main bulkheads, and cabin sole.
		$51,360	The above, plus rough electrical work, unfinished joiner-work, and headliner.
Spencer 51 *aft cock-* *pit (cen-* *ter cock-* *pit also* *avail-*	51′/13′ 2″/7′ 5″ 30,000 lbs. $111,600	$18,580	Hull only. Light displacement hull with large skeg-mounted rudder (not included).
		$41,565	Hull with deck, main

able, *prices* *differ-* *ing)*		$69,959	bulkheads, cabin sole, ballast. Interior needs finishing.
Spencer *1330* *center* *cockpit* *(aft* *cockpit* *also* *avail-* *able)*	44' 4"/13'/7' 24,000 lbs. $91,480	$15,350 $34,115 $69,959	Hull only. Hull with deck, main bulkheads, cabin sole, ballast. Interior needs finishing.

Starrett & Jenks Yacht Co., 1421 Bay Street S.E., St. Petersburg, Florida 33701

Medford Starrett started building this boat in January and, when I spoke to him in June, had eight kit boatbuilders working in his yard: an engineer, computer technician, dentist, businessman, musician, machinist, clerk, and beach bum. Which gives you an idea of the range of interest in kit boats. Why so many in his yard? If anyone is interested, he leases fenced space in the factory area for $49 a month. He also will obtain whatever fittings and equipment you need to complete the boat at ten percent above his cost. A building manual was in the works and should be available soon.

Starrett 45	45' 8"/11'/6' 1" 25,000 lbs. 895 sq. ft. $139,000	$14,900 $29,900 $49,900	Hull, deck, and all six hatches. The above, plus cabin sole, bulkheads, rudder, pedestal steering, ballast, and engine. Interior needs finishing and sails are not included. Sailaway Kit, with rigging, sails, roughed-in interior.

Tylercraft (Chichester Boat Co.), 1439 Montauk Highway, Oakdale, New York 11769
Any Tylercraft boat can be purchased to any stage of construction. Ted Tyler can answer any questions. Their boats are available with twin keels or (as an option) a single keel.

Tyler 26	26′/8′/2′ 7″ 5,400 lbs. 321 sq. ft. $11,995	$7,195	Hull and deck with bulkheads and rudder installed.
Tyler 29	29′ 3″/8′ 8″/2′ 10″ 7,200 lbs. 375 sq. ft. $14,995	$8,395	As above.
Tyler 40	40′/13′/3′ 8″ 22,000 lbs. 750 sq. ft. $54,995	$20,000	As above.

Vineyard Yachts, Inc., Box 1046 (Beach Road), Vineyard Haven, Massachusetts 02568
David C. Thompson, president of Vineyard Yachts, told us, "We'll sell anything from the bare hull to a fully finished boat. In reality, we seldom build half a boat—it's usually just about the whole thing or a hull. We give the hull buyer drawings and dimensions, suggestions as to layout changes and furnish him with everything from screws to fiber glass at our cost plus a handling fee. We don't sell him the hull and kiss him good-bye."

Wasque 26	26′/8′ 8″/2′ 3″ 4,800 lbs. $13,500 to $16,500	$4,650	Bare hull (deck and trunk cabin, $1,975). This and the 32 (below) are semidisplacement hulls with handsome, traditional Down East lines.

Wasque 32	32' 2"/9' 10"/ 2' 6" 7,000–9,000 lbs. $25,000 to $40,000	$5,750	Bare hull (deck and cabin trunk, $1,975).

Webber's Cove Boat Yard, East Blue Hill, Maine 04629

John Cousins, owner of Webber's Cove, introduced bare hulls in 1964 and feels it's a good way to get a boat if your wallet is a little thin. Both the 34 and 40 are traditional Down East-style workboats. About half are sold for commercial use and half finished as pleasure boats. Cousins will finish a boat to any stage of construction.

Down East 34	33' 10"/10' 9½" on request	$6,700	Bare hull. Three dif- ferent deck units are available with the 34- footer. The lobster fisherman deck is $4,300; a sedan cruiser deck is $4,800.
Down East 40	39' 11"/13' 11"/ 4' 4" 14.4 tons on request	$12,000	Bare hull. No decks are available yet for this boat.

Westsail Corp., Box 1828, Costa Mesa, California 92626

Westsail provides construction help through a custom boat department in Costa Mesa, a 400-page construction manual (you can subscribe to periodic revisions for $20 a year), parts lists, and an occasional newsletter for kit builders. The 32 and 42 are both W.I.B. Crealock-designed double-enders. The 32 has more traditional lines, a definite Colin Archer derivation, while the 42 is a more modern design, available with either a center or aft cockpit arrangement. Financing available.

Westsail 32	32'/11'/5' 19,500 lbs. 753 sq. ft. $44,800	$7,500	Bare hull only. (All 32 prices are FOB Costa Mesa or Wrightsville Beach, North Car- olina.)

		$15,750	A bigger package, with deck, ballast, cabin sole, and rudder installed.
		$26,750	Sailaway Kit. This includes spars, rigging, working sails. Belowdecks, there are only structural bulkheads and a temporary ladder.
		$35,500	A semifinished vessel, called the Liveaboard Kit. There are no headliner, no drawers or doors, and only rudimentary equipment (two temporary lights, one-burner stove, etc.) belowdecks.
Westsail 42	42′ 11″/13′/5′ 8″ 31,500 lbs. 1,097 sq. ft. (ketch rig) $84,500	$17,000	Bare hull only. (All 42 and 43 prices are FOB Costa Mesa.)
		$29,950	Deck, ballast, cabin sole, and rudder installed.
		$49,950	Sailaway Kit (see above).
		$66,500	Liveaboard Kit (see above).
Westsail 43	42′ 11″/13′/5′ 8″ 31,500 lbs. 968 sq. ft. (cutter) $91,500	$17,000	Bare hull.
		$31,500	Basic kit with deck, lead ballast, cabin sole, rudder.
		$52,750	Sailaway (see above).
		$69,750	Liveaboard (see above).

The Willard Co., 11200 Condor Avenue, Fountain Valley, California 92708

| *8-Tonner* | 35′ 2″/10′ 6″/ 4′ 8″ 17,000 lbs. 600 sq. ft. $29,950 | $19,950 | Sailaway Kit, complete on the exterior with sails, but bare bones belowdecks, with only the cabin sole and bulkheads installed. This sloop was designed in collaboration with W.I.B. Crealock for long-distance cruising. |

Windward Marine, Inc., 3310 S. Union, Tacoma, Washington 98409 Two of Windward's 50-footers were being worked on by owners when we talked to Harold Stocker, president of the company. He tells us that Windward supplies plans and detailed interior drawings, and can help homebuilders get hardware and other supplies at discount. The 50 was designed by Edwin Monk & Son and, in Stocker's words, "is meant to go to sea."

Searaker 50	50′ 4″/13′ 6″/6′ 4″ 38,000 1,057 sq. ft. (ketch rig) $130,500 (cutter)	$13,600	Hull with four bulkheads (with ballast in place, $18,600).
		$21,500	Hull with cabin sole and fuel and water tanks.
		$28,900	Hull with all the above, plus deck and house, temporarily set in place.
		$35,500	Deck and house permanently secured, hatches, portlights supplied and cut in, cap and rub rails.
		$72,750	Interior joinerwork

installed but not
finished, rough elec-
trical wiring only.
This does not include
deck hardware, spars,
interior oiling, or
painting.

Yacht Constructors, Inc., 7030 N.E. 42nd Avenue, Portland, Oregon 97218

Yacht Constructors has launched about 500 Cascades since its start in 1954 as one of the earliest manufacturers of large fiber-glass hulls. They will finish a boat to any stage of completion, and, should you wish to start with a bare hull, have some tanks, interior fiber-glass modules, and molded cabin/cockpit/deck units to speed the project. They supply detailed plans and instructions and will answer any questions that come up. Joseph Koedel, a Pennsylvanian who spent 1,000 hours finishing a Cascade 36, has some cost figures for us. In late 1973, he bought the hull and deck, then had the builder install bulkheads, engine bed, and floor timbers to be sure the shape of the hull was held correctly. His total completion cost, including rent for a garage to build it in, sail inventory, electronic equipment, etc., was $33,000. He feels that if he had wanted to cut corners, he could have done it for $26,000.

Cascade 29	29'/8' 7"/4' 9" 8,000 lbs. 362 sq. ft. $32,000	$2,500	Bare hull, rudder tube, shaft tube, beam clamp, and set of plans. Equipment list with prices available.
Cascade 36	36' 2"/10'/5' 6" 13,000 lbs. 590 sq. ft. $55,000	$4,290	As above.
Cascade 42	42'/11' 2"/6' 18,450 lbs. 715 sq. ft. $85,000	$5,850	As above.

Yachtcraft (Islander Yachts), 1922 Barranca Road, Irvine, California 92714

Yachtcraft is the kit version of Islander Yachts and it's been operating for about ten years. The company has a good builder aid program worked out through its dealers, supplying construction manuals and plans with their hulls. This division does not supply completed boats, of course.

Yachtcraft 30	30'/10'/5' 8,600 lbs. 429 sq. ft.	$9,421	We've listed the basic kit prices for all the Yachtcraft hulls. This buys the hull, deck bolted on, and rudder. The company also supplies all the components needed for completion and their price lists are available through dealers.
Yachtcraft 34	33' 9"/10' 2"/ 4' 6" 10,400 lbs. 471 sq. ft.	$8,121	This is a traditional cruiser with full keel.
Yachtcraft 37	36' 9"/10' 10"/ 5' 8" 14,000 lbs. 605 sq. ft.	$9,884	Fin-keeled cruiser designed by Bruce King and also available as a motor sailer (both sloop-rigged). The basic motor sailer kit is $10,318.
Yachtcraft 41S	41' 2"/13'/6' 6" 21,900 lbs. 867 sq. ft.	on request	This is a roomy, clipper-bowed sloop.
Yachtcraft 41C	45' 6"/13' 2"/5' 22,000 lbs. 977 sq. ft.	$15,099	Traditional cruising ketch.

Yachtcraft 44	43′ 11″/11′/5′ 10″ 22,500 lbs. 834 sq. ft.	$11,494	A Bill Lapworth-designed cruising sloop with ample room.

INDEX

Page entries in bold type refer to illustrations

ABOUT THE AUTHOR

BONNIE O'BOYLE is an editor at *Motor Boating & Sailing* magazine and has had articles published in *Rudder* magazine, *Cosmopolitan,* and *Seventeen.* This is her first book. She lives in Bristol, Pennsylvania, in a 300-year-old inn.